A REVOLUTION IN KINDNESS

Anita Roddick Books
An Imprint of Anita Roddick Publications Ltd.
93 East Street, Chichester
West Sussex
England PO 19 1HA
www.AnitaRoddick.com

Published by Anita Roddick Books 2003
© 2003 Anita Roddick Publications, Ltd.

Author: Anita Roddick
Editor: Anita Roddick
Copy Editors: Brooke Shelby Biggs,
Linda Weber
Publishing Director: Cal Joy
Consulting Publishing Director:
Justine Roddick
Communications Director: Karen Bishop

Design: Wheelhouse Creative Ltd.
**Thank you Wheelhouse Creative for
another amazingly creative design job.**
www.WheelhouseCreative.co.uk
Illustration: Kary Fisher
at Wheelhouse Creative Ltd.
Cover Design: Kary Fisher

Special thanks to John Owen, Terry Newell
and Chris Hemesath from Weldon Owen, for
their kindness and generosity in producing
this book. www.weldonowen.com

Printed on Recycled Paper

PRINTED IN THE UNITED STATES.

A catalogue record for this book is available
from the British Library.
Distributed in the United Kingdom by Airlift
Book Company www.airlift.co.uk

Distributed in North America
by Red Wheel/Weiser
www.redwheelweiser.com

Distributed in Australia
by HarperCollinsPublishers
www.harpercollins.com.au

A Revolution in Kindness
ISBN: 0-9543959-1-3

03 10 9 8 7 6 5 4 3 2 1

DEDICATED TO
KAREN BISHOP
WHO MAKES EVERYTHING HAPPEN

(KINDLY!)

A REVOLUTION IN KINDNESS ❧

KINDNESS IS A WORD THAT IS USED SO COMMONLY AND SO LIGHTLY. WHAT IS TRUE KINDNESS?

HOW HAS IT DISAPPEARED FROM OUR LIVES WITHOUT OUR NOTICE? YET KINDNESS CAN EMERGE FROM THE MOST HARROWING HELLS THAT HUMAN BEINGS ENDURE, AND IS SO OFTEN THE LAST VESTIGE OF OUR HUMANITY.

THE (UN)HAPPIEST PLACE ON EARTH?

NO MORE SWEATSHOPS

Young women in Bangladesh work 15 hours a day – every day – and endure beatings and threats to their livelihoods. They are paid 5 cents for each Disney shirt they sew.

A new coalition of labor, religious, student, women's, human and civil rights organizations believes that we can end sweatshops – and we can do it before the decade is over. Demand legislation prohibiting goods made by sweatshop and child labor from entering the U.S.

LEARN MORE. SIGN OUR PETITION. DON'T LET DISNEY MICKEY MOUSE AROUND WITH PEOPLE'S LIVES.

YOU CAN MAKE A DIFFERENCE
Sign the petition, send an email, learn more.
Visit www.AbolishSweatshops.org
or AnitaRoddick.com/NoMore

A revolution is taking hold across the globe. Daily news reports tell us of the sweatshops that produce Gap clothing, the child labor that goes into Nike running shoes, and the deplorable demands that are put on the agricultural workers who bring us Starbucks coffee.

Through the work of reporters, photographers, underground investigators, and the testimony of people working in inhuman conditions, accounts of the sad and shocking working and living conditions of people around the world have provoked a humanitarian response.

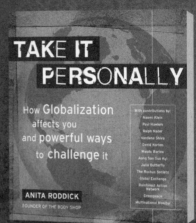

TAKE IT PERSONALLY

How **Globalization** affects you and **powerful ways to challenge it**

A vibrant collection of photographs, essays, montages, and quotes on the driving issues behind globalization from impassioned writers and activist organizations, this is the definitive handbook for the average consumer who wants to learn about the issues and make informed choices.

UK-ISBN:0-00-712898-3   US-ISBN: 1-57324-707-3
Retail Price: U.K. £12.99, U.S. $24.95 (Volume, non-profit, and educational discounts available. Please call for pricing.)
From U.S. telephones: 1-800-423-7087

WHAT WE NEED NOW IS A REVOLUTION IN KINDNESS

REDEFINING KINDNESS

I OFTEN WONDERED, DURING MY TIME WITH THE BODY SHOP, HOW WE COULD MAKE BUSINESS KINDER—WHETHER IT WAS WITHIN THE ORGANIZATION ITSELF OR THE RELATIONSHIP WITH SUPPLIERS AND EMPLOYEES, OR INDEED THE COMMUNITY AT LARGE. MOSTLY I WONDERED HOW TO MEASURE JOY IN THE WORKPLACE. IMPOSSIBLE AND IRRELEVANT, MANY SAID. KINDNESS IN A HIGH-PERFORMANCE ORGANIZATION, ISN'T THAT A BIT LIKE TOSSING A HOT POTATO INTO A COLD BOWL OF WATER, WHERE THE BEST YOU CAN DO IS JUST WARM THINGS UP?

IT WASN'T TRUE. AFTER 26 YEARS OF SHAPING THE SPIRIT OF THE BODY SHOP, I FOUND THAT THE BEST YOU CAN DO IS BETTER THAN YOU EVER IMAGINED.

I FOUND THAT ONCE YOU HAD CHANGED THE LANGUAGE OF BUSINESS FROM ONE WHICH IS PURELY ECONOMIC TO ONE OF REFLECTION AND CARE AND A DEDICATION TO SOCIAL JUSTICE, PEOPLE FELT THEY COULD BRING THEIR HEART TO THE WORKPLACE. THEN AND ONLY THEN DID THE WORKPLACE SHIFT FROM A MONDAY-TO-FRIDAY DEATH TO A MONDAY-TO-FRIDAY SENSE OF FEELING ALIVE.

IT WAS AN AMAZING COUPLE OF DECADES. THOUSANDS OF US WERE EXPERIENCING THIS COMPULSIVE SEARCH FOR CONNECTION, COMMON PURPOSE AND A GROWING SENSE OF FRIENDSHIP. NEIGHBORHOOD AND COMMUNITY SUDDENLY FOUND A SPECIAL PLACE IN THE BUSINESS WORLD.

I FOUND THAT IF A BUSINESS IS MANAGED FROM THE HEART, GREAT THINGS CAN AND WILL HAPPEN. ALL THAT IS STOPPING US IS OUR IMAGINATION.

THAT'S WHY I WANTED TO PUT TOGETHER A BOOK LIKE THIS. IT'S A WORK OF IMAGINATION—IN THE SENSE THAT PEOPLE IN A WIDE VARIETY OF PLACES AND ROLES HAVE IMAGINED WHAT KINDNESS WOULD MEAN IN THE STRUCTURES THEY EXIST WITHIN. BUT, ALTHOUGH THE CONTENTS OF THIS BOOK ARE SUPPOSED TO BE FREE-FORM, UNEX-PECTED AND VARIED—AN INVITATION TO SERENDIPITY—THEY ALSO HAVE A MORE SERIOUS PURPOSE: TO DUST DOWN THE CONCEPT OF KINDNESS AND REVIVE IT.

TO ME, KINDNESS IS ONE OF THE MOST IMPORTANT WORDS IN THE ENGLISH LANGUAGE. IT'S ENORMOUSLY RESONANT AND LIFE-ENHANCING,

AND YET, OVER THE PAST GENERATION OR SO, IT HAS BEGUN TO DISAPPEAR FROM POLITE DISCOURSE. IT'S CONSIDERED INSIPID, ALMOST EMBARRASSING. PEOPLE ARE NOT PRAISED FOR THEIR KINDNESS ANYMORE. IT IS OFTEN VIEWED AS SOMETHING SANCTIMONIOUS, PATRONIZING AND UNREALISTIC—AS IF BEING KIND SOMEHOW IGNORES THE BASIC CAUSES OF A PROBLEM IN THE FIRST PLACE. KINDNESS CARRIES WITH IT IMPLICATIONS OF NOBLESSE OBLIGE, EVEN SNOBBERY.

READING THROUGH THE CONTRIBUTIONS TO THIS BOOK MAKES ME REALIZE THAT KINDNESS IS SIMPLY MISUNDERSTOOD.

ITS POWER COMES FROM ITS OVERWHELMING SIMPLICITY. THE KINDNESS DESCRIBED IN THIS BOOK IS OFTEN ALL TOO AWARE OF THE POLITICAL OR ECONOMIC REALITIES THAT CAUSE PAIN AND TRAGEDY. YET OVER AND OVER AGAIN, WE SEE HOW THE SIMPLE ACT OF REACHING OUT AS ONE HUMAN BEING TO ANOTHER CAN BE A TRULY COURAGEOUS ACT IN THE FACE OF SUCH ODDS.

FURTHER, KINDNESS DOESN'T HAVE TO BE INSIPID OR RANDOM TO BE EFFECTIVE. FAR FROM IT: DELIBERATE KINDNESS CAN BE FIERCE,

TENACIOUS, UNEXPECTED, UNCONDITIONAL AND SOMETIMES POSITIVELY REVOLUTIONARY.

THESE QUALITIES GIVE KINDNESS ITS POWER TO CREATE CHANGE, TO MAKE THINGS HAPPEN. AND IN A PERIOD OF HUMAN HISTORY IN WHICH WE ARE OBSESSED WITH CHANGE—PERSONAL OR POLITICAL—AND ARE UNSURE WHETHER IT IS POSSIBLE AT ALL, KINDNESS COULD BE OUR SALVATION.

ANITA RODDICK OBE

ACTIVIST AND FOUNDER OF THE BODY SHOP

WHAT WOULD THE WORLD LOOK LIKE IF PEOPLE WERE KINDER TO NATURE?

oxygen

IF PEOPLE ACTED AS CARETAKERS TO THE NATURAL WORLD

IF HUMANS ARE TO SURVIVE, WE HAVE TO RE-EMBED OURSELVES IN THE EARTH FAMILY. BEING KIND TO OTHER SPECIES IS BASED ON REALIZING WE ARE ALL KINDRED SPECIES. THIS WOULD REVOLUTIONIZE SCIENCE, TECHNOLOGY, ECONOMICS, POLITICS AND CULTURE.

COMPASSION AND KINDNESS AS THE BASIS OF OUR RELATIONSHIP WITH NONHUMAN FELLOW BEINGS MEANS 'DOING NO HARM.' WE CAN NO LONGER THINK OF 'OWNING' GENES, ORGANISMS, REPRODUCTION BUT INSTEAD RECOGNIZE THAT WE BELONG TO THE WEB OF LIFE AND ARE CO-CREATORS WITH OTHER SPECIES. KINDNESS TO OTHER SPECIES ALSO CREATES A NON-VIOLENT ECONOMY BASED ON SHARING, GIVING AND PROTECTING IN PLACE OF THE CURRENT VIOLENT ECONOMIC SYSTEM OF CORPORATE GLOBALIZATION BASED ON GRABBING, DESTROYING AND PRIVATIZING THE RESOURCES OF THE EARTH, INCLUDING WATER AND BIODIVERSITY.

COMPASSION FOR OTHER SPECIES IS ALSO THE BEST LESSON IN DEEP DEMOCRACY. WHEN ALL BEINGS HAVE RIGHTS AND INTRINSIC WORTH,

DIVERSITY BECOMES A VALUE IN AND OF ITSELF. DIVERSITY BECOMES THE GROUNDS FOR DEMOCRACY—AN EARTH DEMOCRACY.

AND IN A WORLD OF DIVERSITY WHERE ALL BEINGS FLOURISH, CULTURAL DIVERSITY ALSO FLOURISHES. PEACE REPLACES THE 'CLASH OF CIVILIZATIONS,' LOVE REPLACES HATRED, HOPE REPLACES HOPELESSNESS.

WHEN WE RECOGNIZE THAT WE ARE DEPENDENT ON OTHER SPECIES— THE OXYGEN FROM THE TREES, THE FOOD THAT EARTHWORMS AND MILLIONS OF SOIL ORGANISMS PROVIDE FOR US SUSTAINABLY, OUR PARADIGMS SHIFT TO TAKING CARE OF BIODIVERSITY INSTEAD OF WIPING IT OUT IN THE NAME OF PROGRESS AND DEVELOPMENT.

VANDANA SHIVA

ACTIVIST AND PHYSICIST

RESEARCH FOUNDATION FOR SCIENCE, TECHNOLOGY & ECOLOGY

UNCONDITIONAL KINDNESS

SOME SAY THAT CRUELTY IS THE WITHHOLDING OF MERCY—THE OPPOSITE OF KINDNESS. SO KINDNESS IS EXTENDING MERCY TO ALL, PARTICULARLY TO THOSE WHO CANNOT ASK FOR IT. KINDNESS COMES IN ALL SORTS OF SHAPES AND FORMS, BUT TO BE OF TRUE VALUE IT SHOULD BE SELFLESS AND WITHOUT CONDITIONS. UNRESERVED BUT INTELLIGENT. TO BE COMPASSIONATE, KNOWLEDGEABLE AND KIND IS TO BE TRULY WISE.

WILL TRAVERS

CEO, THE BORN FREE FOUNDATION

t

i n

THE BEST PORTION OF A GOOD MAN'S LIFE IS HIS LITTLE,
NAMELESS, UNREMEMBERED ACTS OF KINDNESS AND OF LOVE.

WILLIAM WORDSWORTH

ENGLISH POET

WHAT WOULD A SOCIETY BASED ON KINDNESS LOOK LIKE?

KINDNESS MELTS THE HEART

I'M ON THE CROWDED VICTORIA LINE, HOBBLING IN WITH THE KIND HELP OF A WALKING STICK. AN OLD LADY KINDLY OFFERS ME HER SEAT. I KINDLY THANK HER AND ACCEPT HER OFFER. THE WALKING STICK IS FROM THE FINE TREE THAT PROTECTED ME FROM THE FALLING RAIN, THE RAIN THAT GIVES ITSELF TO TREES AND WEEDS AND FALLS ON RICH AND POOR, SICK AND HEALTHY, GOOD AND BAD. WHAT KIND KINDNESS.

AS THE SUN COMES OUT, IT SMILES AND SHINES AND MISSES NO ONE OR NOTHING, BUT KINDLY SHINES, LIKE THE FALLING SNOW THAT MELTS IN THE HEAT.

OH, THAT KINDLY MAN BACK IN 1979 WHO STUCK A 20-POUND NOTE IN MY TOP POCKET AND WALKED AWAY WITHOUT A THANK YOU. AND THE PEOPLE WHO SAID: "DON'T WORRY ABOUT IT, IT'S NOT YOUR FAULT—WE ALL MAKE MISTAKES, JOHN." PEOPLE HAVE FORGIVEN ME TOO, YOU SEE.

AND THE WOMAN WHO SAID: "YOU CAN SLEEP IN THERE. TAKE THAT KEY, I KNOW YOU'RE SOUND." SHE DID NOT KNOW ME.

I HAVE TO SAY THAT I HAVE BEEN SHOWN UP BY LOVE, KINDNESS AND HONESTY TOO, IN THIS BIG TOWN OF LONDON. AND THE MAN WHO SAID "THERE'S MY HEART AND THERE'S MY MONEY. TAKE WHATEVER YOU PLEASE AND ALL OF IT IF YOU WANT." SO THIS IS IT. MY HEART MELTED UNDERNEATH THE WARMTH OF LOVE AND KINDNESS.

JOHN SHEEHY

VENDOR, *THE BIG ISSUE*
U.K. HOMELESS NEWSPAPER

HAVE YOU BEEN KIND TODAY?

IT STRIKES ME THAT THE 'KINDNESS' FACTOR SEEMS TO BE SADLY OUTMODED IN THIS URBAN AGE OF MUGGINGS AND GRABBINGS. CAN ANYTHING BE DONE TO IMPROVE THE SITUATION? PROBABLY THE ONLY EFFECTIVE RESPONSE IS TO MAKE A START WITH YOURSELF—FROM THE ROOTS UPWARDS, SO TO SPEAK. ASK YOURSELF: HAVE YOU BEEN KIND TODAY? WAS ANYONE KIND TO YOU? HOW DID IT FEEL? WHEN THAT OBNOXIOUS PERSON PUSHED IN FRONT OF YOU IN THE SUPERMARKET QUEUE, DID YOU SPONTANEOUSLY VERBALLY OR PHYSICALLY HEAD-BUTT THEM TO POINT OUT THEIR RUDE BEHAVIOR, OR DID YOU SIMMER IN SILENCE, ONLY TO KICK THE CAR HALF AN HOUR LATER? DID THAT MAKE YOU FEEL BETTER? PROBABLY NOT.

IT CAN BE QUITE A CURIOUS EXERCISE TO TRY TO REACT DIFFERENTLY IN CERTAIN SITUATIONS, JUST TO SEE HOW THE OUTCOME CAN BE AFFECTED. FOR EXAMPLE, WHEN OTHER PEOPLE ARE BEING RUDE OR

AGGRESSIVE, THE MOST OBVIOUS REACTION IS TO TOP THEIR BEHAVIOR BY BEING EVEN MORE VILE IN RETALIATION.

I'M THE FIRST ONE TO ADMIT THAT SOMETIMES IT'S ALMOST IMPOSSIBLE TO PREVENT THIS KIND OF RESPONSE. BUT INTERESTING THINGS START TO HAPPEN WHEN YOU DECIDE TO TAKE CHARGE AND BREAK THIS PATTERN OF DISCONNECTEDNESS BY APPLYING THE KINDNESS FACTOR. WHAT COULD BE A NASTY SITUATION GETS DEFUSED. YOU MAKE CONTACT INSTEAD OF CONFLICT. YOU END UP SMILING INSTEAD OF RAGING.

SO MAKE KINDNESS YOUR DAILY MODUS OPERANDI AND CHANGE YOUR WORLD.

ANNIE LENNOX

SINGER, SONGWRITER AND ACTIVIST

EXPECTING NOTHING IN RETURN

I HAVE TWO FAVORITE PHOTOGRAPHS. ONE IS OF ME BEING KIND: DRAWING SILLY FACES FOR STREET CHILDREN WHO EAGERLY CROWD AROUND ME IN OUR REFUGE IN KATHMANDU. I HAD JUST GOTTEN BACK FROM A MEETING AT THE BRITISH EMBASSY AND NEEDED SOME RELIEF.

BUT WHO WAS BEING KIND TO WHOM? I CERTAINLY NEEDED TO UNWIND, AND THE CHILDREN GAVE ME THE MEANS TO DO SO. EVERY TIME I LOOK AT THAT PHOTO I GET A GREAT SENSE OF THE HAPPINESS THOSE CHILDREN GAVE ME.

THE OTHER PHOTOGRAPH WAS TAKEN AT OUR HIV/AIDS HOSPICE IN JAPA REGION IN THE SOUTHEAST OF NEPAL WHERE WE CARE FOR GIRLS RESCUED FROM FORCED PROSTITUTION. A YOUNG RESIDENT IS TRYING HER HARDEST TO ADD TO MY NEPALESE VOCABULARY. I HAVE KNOWN HER FOR A NUMBER OF YEARS, AND SHE NEVER EXPECTS ANYTHING FROM ME AND IS ALWAYS EXCITED WHEN I ARRIVE, AND SAD WHEN I DEPART. SO ON THAT BASIS, THERE MUST STILL BE GIVING AND TAKING.

THE LAST TIME I SAW HER SHE TOOK A CHARM FROM AROUND HER NECK

AND PLACED IT AROUND MINE. EVERY TIME I LOOK AT THAT PHOTO, I FEEL SAD AND REALIZE I NEED TO DO MORE.

THE GIRL HAS NOTHING AND EVERYTHING—HER INNOCENCE, HER YOUTH, HER HEALTH HAVE BEEN TAKEN FROM HER, BUT KINDNESS IS A MATTER OF NO THOUGHT TO HER. SHE JUST IS. IT SEEMS THE MORE WE HAVE, THE MORE WE EXPECT IN RETURN. THE LESS WE HAVE, THE EASIER IT IS TO GIVE.

TWO YEARS AGO I WAS WORKING IN A HUGE SLUM IN DELHI—MORE THAN 100,000 SOULS, MAINLY RAG-PICKERS, IN THREE-QUARTERS OF A SQUARE MILE OF SQUALID SHANTIES—FROM WHERE A GROWING NUMBER OF CHILDREN ARE ABDUCTED AND SOLD INTO PROSTITUTION. THE DAY BEFORE, THERE HAD BEEN A FIRE— 110 DWELLINGS REDUCED TO ASHES.

I ARRIVED THE FOLLOWING MORNING TO FIND A GROUP OF RESIDENTS WRAPPING FOOD AND CLOTHING IN ANONYMOUS NEWSPAPER PARCELS TO GIVE TO THE VICTIMS AND THEIR FAMILIES. THE SENSE OF

WANTING TO HELP WAS PALPABLE IN THE NARROW LANES. IN RETURN THEY GOT ONLY THE SENSE OF PRIDE IN HELPING OTHERS. WHAT I SAW WAS AN AMAZING SENSE OF COMMUNITY AMONGST THOSE WHO ARE LITERALLY DUMPED ON THE RUBBISH HEAP.

IT REMINDED ME OF A CONVERSATION I HAD HAD THREE WEEKS EARLIER WITH THE CEO OF A LARGE U.K.-BASED MULTINATIONAL. "UNLESS YOU CAN ASSURE US OF SERIOUS PUBLICITY WE HAVE NO SURPLUS FUNDS TO HAND OUT TO CHARITIES," THEY SAID. THEY HAD RECENTLY ANNOUNCED NET PROFITS FOR THE YEAR IN SEVEN FIGURES.

PETER BASHFORD

FOUNDER AND CHAIRMAN
MAITI CHILDREN'S TRUST

KINDNESS HAS NO SELL-BY DATE. IT DOESN'T HAVE TO BE PACKAGED, PERFUMED OR PRETTIFIED. IT IS JUST THE MOST MAGNIFICENT EXPRESSION OF ALL THAT MAKES US WHOLE AND HUMAN. ONLY THE KIND SHOULD BE LISTENED TO IN OUR WORLD.

JOHN BIRD MBE

AUTHOR AND EDITOR-IN-CHIEF, *THE BIG ISSUE*
U.K. HOMELESS NEWSPAPER

RELIEVING THE BURDEN

SHE DIDN'T HAVE MANY POSSESSIONS, BUT EVEN THE ONES SHE HAD IN THE FEW BAGS SHE CARRIED SEEMED TO WEIGH THOUSANDS OF POUNDS AS SHE DRAGGED THEM UP THE COBBLESTONES IN THE RAIN. SHE HADN'T A CLUE WHERE SHE WAS HEADED. ALL SHE KNEW WAS THAT SHE COULDN'T STAY WHERE SHE HAD JUST BEEN—IN THE FLAT OF ANOTHER FALSE FRIEND.

SHE WAS NEARLY DEAF AND BLIND, SO MUCH IN HER MIND. SHE WAS SORE AND NEEDED TO SLEEP. BUT WHERE? OUT OF THE DEADHEADED AIR, A VOICE PIERCED THROUGH TO HER HEART: "LET ME HELP YOU."

SHE TURNED AND SAW A YOUNG GIRL. THE GIRL PICKED UP HALF HER BAGGAGE AND WALKED WITH HER UP THE ROAD. "YOU'RE STRUGGLING WITH IT SO HARD!" SHE SAID, AND THEN ASKED, "DO YOU NEED HELP?"

THE WOMAN ANSWERED WITH THE WORDS STUCK IN HER THROAT. "I NEED TOO MUCH HELP TO ASK FOR. YOU'RE VERY KIND. THANK YOU. THANK YOU FROM MY HEART."

WHAT MATTERED THERE IN THAT MOMENT MOST OF ALL WAS THE HORRIBLE HEAVINESS. IT WAS GONE NOW, LESSENED BY SOMEONE WHO SINCERELY CARED. AND BECAUSE THE GIRL CARED, BECAUSE THE WOMAN COULD SEE IT IN THE GIRL'S EYES, THE WOMAN KNEW THAT SHE TOO MUST TELL THE TRUTH. AND SO SHE DID. AND SO THEY WENT THEIR SEPARATE WAYS, AND THE ROAD WAS EASIER TO WALK ON.

PAMELA

VENDOR, *THE BIG ISSUE*
U.K. HOMELESS NEWSPAPER

MANCHESTER MISADVENTURE

I REMEMBER A COLD NIGHT IN MANCHESTER 20 YEARS AGO. I WAS ON A FIRST DATE AND DRESSED TO IMPRESS. I WAS WEARING MY BEST DESIGNER SUIT AND SHOES AND HAD BOOKED THE MOST EXPENSIVE RESTAURANT IN TOWN TO WINE AND DINE MY BEAUTIFUL COMPANION. THE EVENING WAS GREAT AND, WITH THE PROMISE OF A SECOND DATE, I GALLANTLY TOOK MY DATE HOME. IT WAS AT THIS POINT THAT I REALIZED I HAD JUST ENOUGH MONEY TO TAKE A TAXI TO MY BEST FRIEND'S HOUSE.

I KNOCKED ON THE DOOR, THERE WAS NO REPLY. I KNOCKED AGAIN AND AGAIN. LITTLE DID I KNOW HE WAS 200 MILES AWAY IN LONDON. I DECIDED TO TRY TO ENTER THROUGH A WINDOW. SUDDENLY AN ALARM SOUNDED, LIGHTS WENT ON IN THE STREET AND DOGS BARKED. I PANICKED, AFRAID OF BEING ACCUSED A BURGLAR, AND RAN ACROSS A MUDDY FIELD, EVENTUALLY FINDING A MAIN ROAD AND A TAXI. THE DRIVER TOOK PITY ON ME AND TOOK ME INTO THE CITY CENTER FOR THE 2 POUNDS I HAD LEFT AFTER AN EXPENSIVE EVENING.

NOW I WAS STRANDED IN THE CENTER OF THE CITY AT 3A.M. I WAS COLD AND TIRED, AND THE STREET WAS DESERTED. I DECIDED TO STAY UNDER THE SHELTER OF A NEARBY BUS STOP, AND IT WAS THERE THAT I MET TOM,

A DOWN-AND-OUT, TRAMP, HOMELESS PERSON, WHATEVER LABEL WE PUT ON THESE FELLOW HUMAN BEINGS. AT FIRST I AVOIDED HIM AS I ALWAYS DID THE HOMELESS. HERE I WAS IN A DESIGNER SUIT AND EXPENSIVE COLOGNE NEXT TO SOMEONE WITH A BLANKET UNDER HIS ARM WHO LOOKED LIKE 20 MILES OF ROUGH ROAD.

HE ASKED ME FOR MONEY, AND I SAID I DIDN'T HAVE ANY BUT I FELT HE DESERVED AN EXPLANATION. TOM LAUGHED WHEN I TOLD HIM ABOUT MY MISADVENTURE. I LAUGHED WITH HIM. HE THEN TOOK SOME COINS FROM HIS POCKET AND LEFT. FIVE MINUTES LATER, HE CAME BACK WITH COFFEE FOR ME. HERE WE WERE, I IN MY EXPENSIVE CLOTHES AND HE WITH NOTHING, BROUGHT TOGETHER BY A SIMPLE ACT OF KINDNESS.

I OFTEN LOOKED FOR TOM, TO RETURN THE GESTURE, BUT I NEVER FOUND HIM. I WANTED TO DO MORE THAN GIVE HIM MONEY. I WANTED TO SHAKE HIS HAND AND TREAT HIM WITH THE RESPECT AND DIGNITY HE DESERVED. HE TAUGHT ME AN IMPORTANT LESSON THAT NIGHT, ONE I HAVE NEVER FORGOTTEN.

ROB CAPRINI-WOOD

REFUGEE SKILLS DEVELOPER

THE KINDNESS OF STRANGERS

NONSTOP RAIN SOAKING INTO MY SKIN. IT FEELS LIKE IT HAS BEEN RAINING FOREVER, ALTHOUGH ITS ACTUALLY ONLY BEEN TWO DAYS. TWO DAYS OF RAIN IS A LOT TO COPE WITH WHEN YOU'RE SLEEPING OUTSIDE. MY CLOTHES ARE SO DAMP THEY ARE STICKING TO ME, AND MY SLEEPING BAG IS DRENCHED. I SHRINK FURTHER BACK INTO THE DOORWAY, TRYING TO KEEP OUT OF THE WAY OF THE RELENTLESS RAIN. THE WORST THING ABOUT BEING HOMELESS IS THE WAY THE HOURS AND THE DAYS JUST SEEM TO DRAG. I CAN GET A HOT MEAL WHEN THE DAY CENTER OPENS, BUT THAT'S ANOTHER THREE HOURS AWAY YET.

NORMALLY I WOULD GO AND SIT IN THE LIBRARY, KEEP WARM AND READ THE NEWSPAPERS, BUT NOT TODAY. TODAY IS WEDNESDAY, AND THE LIBRARY IS CLOSED ALL DAY. THERE IS NOTHING I CAN DO BUT TRY AND SHELTER IN THIS DOORWAY UNTIL THE DAY CENTER OPENS.

AS I SIT, HUDDLED UP AND SHIVERING, I NOTICE SOMEONE HAS STOPPED IN FRONT OF THE DOORWAY. IT IS A YOUNG WOMAN PUSHING A BUGGY. IN THE BUGGY IS A SMALL BOY AGED AROUND TWO. AS I LOOK

AT HIM, HE FLASHES ME THE MOST ENORMOUS BEAMING SMILE. AT THE SAME TIME, THE RAIN EASES OFF. I KNOW IT'S CRAZY, BUT IT'S ALMOST AS IF THE TWO EVENTS ARE LINKED. THE WOMAN ASKS ME IF I AM OKAY, AND HANDS ME A CARRIER BAG CONTAINING A LEAFLET ABOUT GOD, AND SOME SANDWICHES AND CRISPS. BEFORE SHE WALKS AWAY SHE PUTS A TWO-POUND COIN INTO MY HAND.

SOMEHOW, IN THE LAST FEW MINUTES, MY AFTERNOON HAS GOT A WHOLE LOT BETTER. I DECIDE TO WALK TO THE CAFÉ, AND USE THE MONEY TO BUY MYSELF AN HOUR IN THE WARM DRINKING TEA. AS I WALK DOWN THE ROAD THE RAIN FINALLY STOPS.

SAM

VENDOR, *THE BIG ISSUE*
U.K. HOMELESS NEWSPAPER

THE STRANGE FRUIT OF KINDNESS

KINDNESS, IF DEFINED AS ANY CLOSE RELATIVE TO MERE TOLERANCE, IS A VERY LEAKY BOAT. REAL KINDNESS IS BUILT UP ON ACTUAL DELIGHT IN THE OTHER.

JUST WHO HAVE BEEN OUR STREET OUTCASTS, OUR LOCAL WEIRDOS, FREAKS, ECCENTRICS, ALCOHOLICS AND DRUG ABUSERS? HERE IN BALTIMORE, MARYLAND, THOSE LABELS COULD WELL HAVE DEFINED SOME OF OUR GREATEST LOCAL HEROES—WRITER AND POET EDGAR ALAN POE; JOHNS HOPKINS HOSPITAL'S GREATEST SURGEON (AND MORPHINE ADDICT) DR. WILLIAM S. HALSTED; SOULFUL AND DOWN-TRODDEN BILLIE HOLIDAY; OR MORE RECENTLY, THE LATE TRANSVESTITE DIVINE AND HIS BEST FRIEND, DIRECTOR JOHN WATERS.

NOW CONTEMPLATE HOW MANY UNIQUE VOICES LIKE HOLIDAY'S AND SCIENTIFIC TALENTS LIKE HALSTED'S LANGUISH TODAY, SILENCED IN

AMERICA'S EVER-GROWING PRISONS—AN AMERICA THAT NOW HAS
A GREATER PERCENTAGE OF ITS PEOPLE IN PRISON THAN DOES
RUSSIA. SUCH A TRAGIC WASTE, PARTICULARLY AS WE ARE FAST
LEARNING THAT URBAN REDEVELOPMENT IS BEST QUICKENED BY
EMBRACE OF 'THE CREATIVE CLASS'—THAT CITIES WITH STRONG ARTS,
ROCK AND GAY SCENES FLOURISH IN DIRECT PROPORTION TO THEIR
INCLUSIONARY WELCOME OF THE WILDLY DIVERSE. REAL KINDNESS IS
MOUTH-GAPING RESPECT AND COMPASSION FOR JUST HOW HARD IT IS
TO BE A HUMAN BEING—ANY HUMAN BEING.

REBECCA ALBAN HOFFBERGER

FOUNDER AND DIRECTOR
THE AMERICAN VISIONARY ART MUSEUM

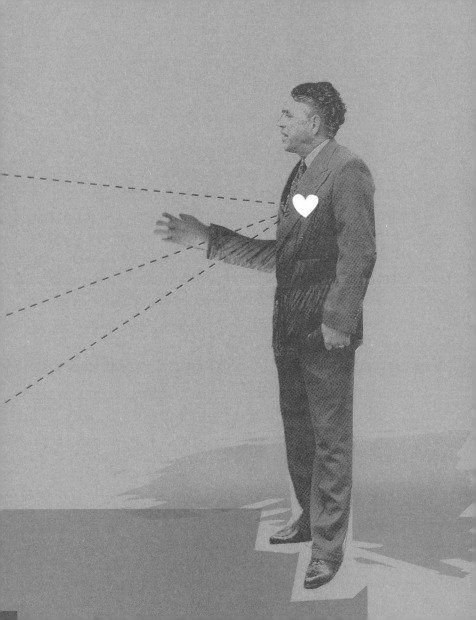

AN ACT OF MERCY

LEMA, TOGETHER WITH SEVERAL OTHER BOYS FROM HIS VILLAGE, WAS KIDNAPPED BY A PLATOON FROM AN INCURSIVE ARMY. ALONG THE JOURNEY, THE BOYS WERE BEATEN AND TERRORIZED. AS THEY APPROACHED A RIVER, THE CONVOY WAS STRAFED BY A HELICOPTER GUNSHIP, AND MOST OF THE CAPTORS WERE KILLED. ALL THE BOYS RAN TO SAFETY, BUT LEMA STAYED WITH NUMKE, ONE OF HIS INJURED CAPTORS, AND HELPED NURSE HIS WOUNDS. DESPITE THE FACT THAT THIS MAN HAD TORMENTED HIM, LEMA WAS ABLE TO SEE NUMKE AS A HUMAN BEING. FILLED WITH COMPASSION, LEMA HELPED NUMKE REACH THE MISSIONARY FIELD HOSPITAL.

THIS IS KINDNESS. HUMAN KINDNESS SHINES LIKE BLAZING TORCHES. KINDNESS IS AN ACT OF MERCY GIVEN AWAY RESPONSIBLY BY A PERSON WHO HAS EVERY RIGHT TO EXPRESS WRATH.

ALWYN PEREIRA

SOCIAL ENTREPRENEUR AND CEO
YOUTH ENTERTAINMENT STUDIOS, UNITED KINGDOM

KINDNESS IS PROFITABLE

DURING THE YEARS I SPENT RESEARCHING THE BOOK *FALLEN ANGELS: THE SEX WORKERS OF SOUTH ASIA*, I FOUND KINDNESS IN PLACES OF THE MOST HORRIBLE CRUELTY. IT CHANGED MY LIFE, WHEN I HAD THOUGHT I KNEW IT ALL.

AGAIN AND AGAIN, AS I SAT IN THE BROTHELS WITH THE GIRLS AS THEY TOLD ME ABOUT THEIR LIVES, THEY WOULD SUDDENLY SMILE, REFLECTING ON A MOMENT OF KINDNESS IN THEIR YEARS OF HELL. A BROTHEL MADAME COMFORTING A CHILD WHO'D BEEN BEATEN FOR REFUSING TO SELL HER BODY. A CLIENT WHO WOULD COME OFTEN TO THE BROTHEL TO HIRE A YOUNG GIRL, AND IN THE PRIVACY OF THE BEDROOM WOULD REFUSE SEX, AND SHARE SWEETS AND STORIES WITH HER. A TRAFFICKER WITH VICTIM IN HAND, WHO WOULD CHANGE HIS MIND AND PUT THE GIRL ON THE BUS BACK HOME.

IN OUR WAR AGAINST SEXUAL EXPLOITATION IN ASIA, KIND PEOPLE INSIDE BROTHELS ARE BECOMING INFILTRATORS AND RESISTANCE FIGHTERS. IN THE NEW PHASE OF THE WAR—DIRECTLY ADDRESSING THE 'DEMAND SIDE' OF CLIENTS, MADAMES AND PIMPS—KINDNESS WILL BE OUR STRONGEST WEAPON. THE ATTITUDES FOR CHANGE ARE THERE

WITHIN THE BROTHELS, AND THOSE ATTITUDES ARE ROOTED IN BASIC HUMAN KINDNESS. OUR WORK IS TO CULTIVATE THOSE ATTITUDES AND REDUCE THE DEMAND FOR 'EXPLOITED GOODS.'

PROSTITUTES, MADAMES AND CLIENTS THEMSELVES MUST BE THE AGENTS OF CHANGE. THOSE WHO CAN LEAD THE CHANGE ARE THOSE WHO CAN BE MOTIVATED BY KINDNESS, AND WHO—LET'S BE REALISTIC—UNDERSTAND THAT OPPRESSION AND CRUELTY, LIKE HIV AND AIDS, MAKE FOR BAD SEX AND BAD BUSINESS. WE CAN MOBILIZE INDIVIDUALS BY HELPING THEM TO ASSERT THE POWER OF KINDNESS, AND HELPING THEM TO SHOW OTHER CLIENTS, PROSTITUTES AND MADAMES THE BENEFITS OF KINDNESS.

IT'S A TOUGH WORLD IN THE BROTHELS. OUR GOAL ISN'T TO SPREAD SWEETNESS AND LIGHT. OUR GOAL IS TO CONVINCE PEOPLE THAT KINDNESS IS MORE PROFITABLE THAN CRUELTY.

JOHN FREDERICK
DIRECTOR, RAY OF HOPE
KATHMANDU, NEPAL

LOVE THY ENEMY

IT IS EASY TO BE KIND TO PEOPLE WHO ARE KIND TO US, TO PEOPLE WHO RADIATE SURPLUS ENERGY AND GOODWILL AND TO PEOPLE WHOM WE LIKE. BUT WHAT WOULD THE WORLD LOOK LIKE IF WE WERE TO TRY BEING KIND TO OUR ENEMIES, TO PEOPLE WHO HAVE BEEN DEEPLY SCARRED OR MARGINALIZED IN THEIR UPBRINGING, TO PEOPLE WE DON'T LIKE OR WHO WE HAVE EVERY REASON TO FEAR?

AS A TRAVELER, I HAVE HAD A CHANCE TO TRY THAT OUT THROUGH MY LONG-STANDING POLICY OF SAYING YES TO EVERYONE I MEET ON MY WAY—WITHOUT EXCEPTION. TO SAY "NO"—TO TURN YOUR BACK ON EVEN A SINGLE INDIVIDUAL, IS TO PARTICIPATE IN THE SYSTEMATIC MARGINALIZATION OF HUMAN BEINGS.

SAYING YES TO THE PEOPLE YOU MEET CAN, ON THE FACE OF IT. RESEMBLE A KIND OF SELFLESS GENEROSITY OF A NEIGHBOR, LIKE THE GOOD SAMARITAN. BUT THE STARTING POINT IS AND SHOULD ALWAYS BE ONE'S OWN SELFISH INTEREST: YOU SIMPLY DENY YOURSELF IN

VALUABLE ADVENTURES BY SAYING NO TO PEOPLE WHO CHALLENGE YOU. YOU DENY YOURSELF, PERHAPS OUT OF A FEAR FOR YOUR PERSONAL SAFETY. BUT THESE ARE THE BARRIERS THAT DIVIDE US.

DISPLAYING KINDNESS AND OPENNESS TOWARD THE VERY PEOPLE WHO DIRECTLY CHALLENGE OR FRIGHTEN US IS SIMPLY THE BEST WAY TO GUARANTEE OUR OWN SURVIVAL.

THERE IS NOT A SINGLE PERSON IN THE WORLD YOU NEED TO BE AFRAID OF. (CARS YOU NEED TO WATCH OUT FOR, BUT NOT PEOPLE.) EARLY ON IN MY TRAVELS, I BEGAN TO FREE MYSELF FROM A PARALYZING FEAR OF "OTHERNESS." SINCE THEN IT HAS BEEN A TRUE MIRACLE TO TRAVEL. ALL THE POSITIVE TIME I SPENT WITH THE MANY INHABITANTS OF GHETTOS HAS HELPED ME TO SEE THE HUMANITY BEHIND THE THREAT.

WHEN YOU STOP FEARING OTHERS, THE DOORS OPEN UP FOR YOU TO A UNIVERSE TRULY WITHOUT BORDERS. TO SHOW PEOPLE TRUST IS TO

DECLARE YOUR LOVE. ALL PEOPLE ARE STARVING FOR LOVE AND AFFECTION, EVEN THE MOST DANGEROUS OR THREATENING PEOPLE WHO ARE HELD CAPTIVE BY A HUNGER FOR LOVE.

IF WE ARE TO CREATE A WORLD WITHOUT CRIME AND TERRORISM, WE MUST EMBRACE THE ANGER BEHIND IT ALL, TO TRY TO BE KIND TO THE MARGINALIZED PEOPLE OF THE WORLD RATHER THAN FURTHER MARGINALIZING THEM WITH OUR UNFOUNDED FEARS OF THEM.

JACOB HOLDT

DANISH VAGABOND AND PHOTOGRAPHER

KINDNESS: A DOUBLE-EDGED SWORD

IF YOU SEE A FRIEND AND YOU KNOW HE'S SKINT, YOU OFFER HIM MONEY, BECAUSE SOONER OR LATER YOU GET IT BACK.

GIVING UP YOUR SEAT ON THE BUS IS KINDNESS, BUT IT IS THE KINDNESS THAT IS DECORUM, THE POLITE THING TO DO. KINDNESS IS LIKE SUGAR, A LITTLE IS NICE, BUT TOO MUCH IS TOO SICKLY AND SWEET.

"WOULD YOU LIKE A HAND WITH THAT BAG?"

"NO THANK YOU, I CAN MANAGE."

BUT THAT DOESN'T STOP THEM. "HERE, LET ME."

IT IS AN INVASION, A PAIN IN THE ARSE. KINDNESS CAN ALSO BE A THINLY VEILED FORM OF BULLYING. "GO ON HAVE ANOTHER DRINK!" BUT YOU REFUSE. THEY OFFER AGAIN, BUT YOU STILL REFUSE. THE NEXT THING YOU KNOW YOU GET BULLIED INTO GETTING PISSED. I SHOULD KNOW IT'S HAPPENED ENOUGH TIMES TO ME. KINDNESS CAN REALLY SUCK.

JOHN C

VENDOR, *THE BIG ISSUE*
U.K. HOMELESS NEWSPAPER

KINDNESS AND COMPASSION

JON IS A 32-YEAR-OLD HOMELESS MAN WHO HAD NEVER BEEN SHOWN ANY KINDNESS IN HIS LIFE. HIS FATHER SMASHED BOTH HIS KNEECAPS WITH A HAMMER WHEN HE WAS SIX, AFTER WHICH HIS LIFE SPIRALED OUT OF CONTROL. THE LESS ABLE HE WAS TO COPE, THE MORE INTOL-ERANT AND JUDGMENTAL THE WORLD AROUND HIM BECAME.

WHEN HE FIRST CAME TO OUR CHRISTMAS SHELTER, HE WAS ANGRY AND HURT—A LOST SOUL. BUT THE UNCONDITIONAL LOVE HE RECEIVED FROM HUNDREDS OF VOLUNTEERS, WHO HAD GIVEN UP THEIR CHRISTMAS TO CREATE A COMMUNITY OF KINDNESS, TOUCHED HIM IN A MOST UNEXPECTED WAY. IT GAVE HIM FAITH IN HIMSELF AND THE DETERMINATION TO CONFRONT HIS PROBLEMS AND MOVE FORWARD.

I IMAGINE A WORLD OF KINDNESS TO BE A PLACE WHERE IT IS CHRISTMAS 365 DAYS OF THE YEAR—WHERE THE MAGIC CAST BY OUR VOLUNTEERS IS FOUND EVERYWHERE, EVERY DAY, AND COMPASSION

IS THE UNIVERSAL RESPONSE TO HOMELESSNESS. THE HOPE THAT OUR CHRISTMAS EVENT BROUGHT TO JON'S LIFE WOULD BE DELIVERED TO EVERY HOMELESS PERSON.

IT WOULD BE NÄIVE TO BELIEVE THAT COMPASSION ALONE WILL SOLVE HOMELESSNESS. THERE IS NO DOUBT THAT STRUCTURAL SOLUTIONS, SUCH AS HOUSING AND BENEFITS, ARE CRITICAL. BUT IN ISOLATION THEY ARE MEANINGLESS. HOMELESSNESS IS A LONG AND PAINFUL JOURNEY FRAUGHT WITH HARDSHIPS, AND TIME AND TIME AGAIN, IT IS KINDNESS, CARING AND FRIENDSHIP THAT CARRY HOMELESS PEOPLE THROUGH THEIR BLACKEST AND MOST DIFFICULT DAYS.

SHAKS GHOSH

CHIEF EXECUTIVE OF CRISIS

WHAT WOULD THE HEALTH SYSTEM BE LIKE IF IT WERE KINDER?

A KINDER, GENTLER HEALTH SYSTEM

I AM INFLUENCED BY PER FUGELLI, PROFESSOR OF SOCIAL MEDICINE AT OSLO UNIVERSITY, WHO HAS WRITTEN ON THE ROLE OF TRUST IN MEDICINE. IT OCCURRED TO ME THAT HIS PRESCRIPTION, IF ADOPTED, COULD ENHANCE THE LEVEL OF KINDNESS, IN ADDITION TO INCREAS-ING TRUST WITHIN BRITAIN'S NATIONAL HEALTH SERVICE.

RESPECT BETWEEN INDIVIDUALS WOULD BE A PREREQUISITE. HEALTH PROFESSIONALS MUST SHARE DECISION-MAKING WITH PATIENTS AND RESPECT FOR THEIR AUTONOMY. THIS CAN PREVENT THOSE IN THE MEDICAL FIELD FROM BEING PATRONIZING AND PRESUMPTUOUS, OR OTHERWISE MISUSING THEIR AUTHORITY UNDER THE GUISE OF KINDNESS. IT HAS BEEN HYPOTHESIZED THAT THE DOCTOR-CUM-MASS-MURDERER HAROLD SHIPMAN MIGHT HAVE CONSIDERED THAT KILLING HIS PATIENTS WAS "DOING THEM A KINDNESS."

REALISM IS INCREASINGLY IMPORTANT FOR A POPULATION THAT HAS INFINITE ACCESS TO INFORMATION WITHOUT KNOWLEDGE AND EXPECTATIONS TO MATCH. BOTH ORTHODOX AND COMPLEMENTARY MEDICINES ARE OFTEN GUILTY OF OVERSTATING THEIR OWN EFFECTIVE-NESS—A FORM OF MISPLACED KINDNESS OR OF UNKIND COMMERCIALISM. KINDNESS MAY INVOLVE A HUMANELY DELIVERED EXPLANATION TO A

SICK PATIENT THAT TREATMENT FOR HIS OR HER CONDITION SHOULD CONCENTRATE ON PALLIATION RATHER THAN CURE.

THE LAST ELEMENT, PERHAPS THE MOST OBVIOUS IN THE CONTEXT OF KINDNESS, IS COMPASSION. BRITAIN'S NATIONAL HEALTH SERVICE CAN BE VIEWED AS A FORM OF COLLECTIVE STATE KINDNESS—THE REAL-IZATION THAT WE ARE ALL SUBJECT TO ILLNESS, THAT WHEN ILL, WE ARE ALL VULNERABLE. YET PEOPLE RETURNING FROM THE PRIVATE SECTOR FREQUENTLY REPORT THAT THEY FELT VALUED BY THE PROFES-SIONALS THEY ENCOUNTERED, WHEREAS IN THE NHS THEY FEEL A BURDEN.

STILL, THE ABILITY TO EMPATHIZE—TO PUT ONESELF METAPHORICALLY IN THE PATIENT'S POSITION—COSTS NOTHING. BREAKING BAD NEWS BRUTALLY OR PEDANTICALLY RECITING THE LIMITATIONS OF ONE'S PRO-FESSIONAL BOUNDARIES SERVES TO UNDERMINE BOTH THE GENEROUS VISION OF THE NHS AND THE ESTEEM IN WHICH IT CONTINUES TO BE HELD. PUT TOGETHER, THESE ARE A COMPLICATED PRESCRIPTION. BUT IF OUR COMPLIANCE WERE BETTER, WE COULD ACHIEVE A KINDER, GENTLER HEALTH-CARE SYSTEM.

DAVID TOVEY   **GENERAL PRACTITIONER, UNITED KINGDOM**

EXEMPLARY KINDNESS

MOTHER THERESA SAID "KIND WORDS CAN BE SHORT AND EASY TO SPEAK, BUT THEIR ECHOES ARE TRULY ENDLESS." SHE WAS A WOMAN WHOSE EXAMPLES OF KINDNESS TRULY ECHOED AROUND THE WORLD INSPIRING COMPASSION AND ALTRUISM IN OTHERS.

ANGELINA JOLIE   **ACTRESS AND UNITED NATIONS REFUGEE AGENCY GOODWILL AMBASSADOR**

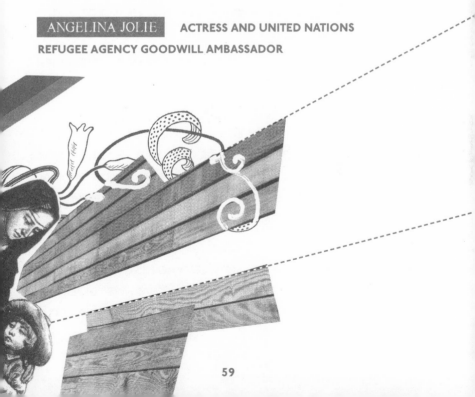

SURROUNDED BY LOVE, NOT MACHINES

ISN'T THE TIME OF LIFE WHEN YOU NEED YOUR LOVED ONES TO BE THE KINDEST AND BRAVEST ACTUALLY THE TIME OF YOUR DEATH? YET MANY OF US DIE IN IMPERSONAL HOSPITALS IN THE PRESENCE OF STRANGERS WHO ARE PAID TO BE THERE, SURROUNDED BY BEEPING MONITORS, IN SHARED ROOMS, CONSTANTLY DISTRACTED AND INTERRUPTED BY THE HOSPITAL ROUTINE.

MEDICAL AND HOSPICE PROFESSIONALS ARE INVALUABLE WHEN NECESSARY, BUT THE ONE THING THAT A HOSPITAL AND THOSE WHO WORK THERE CANNOT PROVIDE IS LOVE.

WHEN DID OUR CLiNICAL NEEDS BECOME MORE IMPORTANT THAN OUR EMOTIONAL AND SPIRITUAL NEEDS? FOR CENTURIES, THE DYING WERE CARED FOR AT HOME BY FAMILY, SURROUNDED BY LOVE. IF MEDICAL NEEDS CANNOT BE MET BY PROFESSIONALS, IF DEATH IS INEVITABLE, WOULDN'T IT BE MORE COMFORTABLE AND BETTER TO DIE AT HOME? ISN'T THAT TRULY KINDER?

THE CONCEPT OF DEATH IS SO OVERWHELMING AND WE ARE SO UNPREPARED FOR THE EXPERIENCE THAT WE DEFER TO PROFESSIONALS. LIKE GIVING BIRTH, DEATH HAS BEEN TURNED INTO A

LESS-THAN-NATURAL EVENT. A HOSPITAL AND ITS STAFF CAN PROVIDE PAIN RELIEF AND PROLONG OR SHORTEN THE PROCESS, BUT AS DEATH INEVITABLY APPROACHES, WHY NOT BE WHERE YOU ARE EMOTIONALLY COMFORTABLE AT A TIME WHEN YOU WILL RELY ON YOUR SOUL AND SPIRIT MORE THAN EVER BEFORE? THE ANSWER IS OFTEN THAT THOSE WHO LOVE US ARE AFRAID THEY CAN'T HANDLE IT, THAT THEY DON'T HAVE THE EMOTIONAL RESOURCES TO DISPENSE KINDNESS AND LOVE WHILE FACING THEIR INEVITABLE LOSS.

BUT ALTHOUGH DEATH IS A LOSS, IT IS ALSO A GIFT: IT GIVES US THE OPPORTUNITY TO SHOW UNWAVERING, BRAVE AND NURTURING LOVE. WHEN FACED WITH THE QUESTION OF HOW TO CARE FOR SOMEONE WHO IS DYING, WE SHOULD ASK OURSELVES WHAT WOULD TRULY SERVE ALL THE NEEDS OF THAT PERSON, NOT JUST THE MEDICAL ONES. WHAT WOULD WE WANT FOR OURSELVES, AND WHAT ARE WE REALLY CAPABLE OF? IT IS AN OPPORTUNITY TO LIVE, LOVE AND LOSE WITH PASSION, COMMITMENT, AND REAL KINDNESS.

KATE MAHER-PURCELL

WIDOW OF GREG, WHO DIED SURROUNDED BY LOVE

WHAT PRICE HEALTH CARE?

KINDNESS IS ABOUT HONESTY—TELLING THE TRUTH, DOING YOUR BEST AND TRYING TO OFFER SOME HOPE WHEN IT'S ALL BUT HOPELESS. KINDNESS IS ABOUT BEING COMFORTABLE WITH UNCERTAINTY AND ABLE TO SHARE THAT WITH YOUR PATIENT. IF YOU TELL THE TRUTH, PATIENTS BEGIN TO MANAGE THEIR—AND YOUR—UNCERTAINTIES AND THE RELATIONSHIP DEEPENS.

ARE WE HONEST AND TRUTHFUL TO PEOPLE IN OUR COUNTRY, AND IN OTHERS? HOW MANY GOVERNMENTS DECLARE HEALTH CARE TO BE A PRIORITY, THEN FAIL TO INVEST IN IT? POOR HOUSING, POOR EDUCATION, INDUSTRIAL PROLIFERATION FOR PROFIT AND CORRUP-TION ARE ALL EVIDENCE OF OUR FAILING COMMITMENT. MASSIVE PHARMACEUTICAL COMPANIES DEFEND THEIR MARKET SHARE, OFFER NO CHEAP DRUGS FOR THE THIRD WORLD, AND CONTRIBUTE TO THE DECIMATION OF CENTRAL AFRICA. THIS DOESN'T SEEM KIND.

KINDNESS HELPS PEOPLE MAKE CHOICES REGARDING THEIR OWN ILLNESS AND TREATMENT OR, AS CITIZENS, DECIDE WHETHER THEY WANT TO BE PART OF A NATION INVESTING IN HEALTH. HOW MUCH KINDNESS AND HONESTY HAVE WE SEEN FROM GOVERNMENTS TRYING TO ENGAGE PEOPLE IN THIS DIFFICULT DEBATE? HEALTH CARE IS NOT CHEAP AND RATIONALIZATION DEBATES ABOUT THE RESOURCES WE ARE WILLING TO DEVITE TO IT ARE UNCOMFORTABLE. IF WE CAN TRY TO BE HONEST WITH OUR PATIENTS ABOUT CHOICES, WHY CAN'T WE DO IT FOR OUR PEOPLE?

PETER LUCE

HOSPITAL MEDICAL DIRECTOR
UNITED KINGDOM

I PREFER YOU TO MAKE MISTAKES IN KINDNESS THAN WORK MIRACLES IN UNKINDNESS.

MOTHER TERESA OF CALCUTTA

Kindness

KINDNESS

kindnes
kindines

kindness
kidnness

COMPASSIONATE CARE

IN HOSPICE CARE WE WORK WITH PEOPLE FACING THE LOSS OF EVERY-
THING THAT MATTERS TO THEM. THEIR BODIES LET THEM DOWN, THEIR
APPEARANCE MAY CHANGE IN WAYS THEY HATE AND YET CANNOT
CONTROL. JOBS HAVE TO BE GIVEN UP, FINANCIAL SECURITY IS
THREATENED. PARENTS CANNOT GIVE THEIR CHILDREN A CUDDLE
BECAUSE IT PHYSICALLY HURTS. PATIENTS LOSE STATUS, CONFIDENCE,
AND DIGNITY. THE FUTURE CANNOT BE PLANNED.

WHEN YOU ARE ILL, YOUR SOCIAL CIRCLE SHRINKS. MANY LOSE SIGHT
OF YOU. THEY SEE INSTEAD THE BEARER OF THIS AWFUL, MUTILATING
CONDITION, WHO MUST EITHER BE AVOIDED OR SMOTHERED IN
KINDNESS. YOU ARE TALKED DOWN TO AND DEALT WITH AS IF YOU HAD
LOST ALL INTELLIGENCE AND HAVE LEFT BEHIND A LIFE'S EXPERIENCE SO
PAINFULLY ASSEMBLED. YOU FACE DREADFUL CHOICES: HOPES ARE
BUILT UP AND DASHED WITH GREAT RAPIDITY.

THE HOSPICE PROJECT IS ABOUT HELPING A PATIENT RECOVER A SENSE
OF SELF IN THE FACE OF OVERWHELMING THREAT. BEING ABLE
TO GIVE PEOPLE TIME IS NOT AN OPTIONAL LUXURY HERE, BUT A BASIC
TOOL. BECAUSE WHAT WE ARE AFTER IS NOT A SOLUTION TO A

PROBLEM, BUT HELPING AN INDIVIDUAL FEEL INTACT IN THE FACE OF DIZZYING, EVER-ACCELERATING CHANGE.

IT DEMANDS A LOT OF THE HEALTH CARE PROFESSIONAL. IT REQUIRES GREAT SKILL IN CONTROLLING SYMPTOMS AND UNDERSTANDING ILLNESS. BUT ABOVE ALL, IT REQUIRES A PARTICULARLY ROBUST KIND OF COMPASSION. THIS IS THE ESSENCE OF KINDNESS, TO KNOW WHEN TO ENVELOPE SOMEONE IN CARE, AND WHEN TO GENTLY CHALLENGE HIM OR PROD HER FORWARD. ONE HAS TO BE ABLE TO UNFLINCHINGLY FACE ANOTHER'S OVERWHELMING FEAR AND TO SHARE SOLEMN MOMENTS WITHOUT EMBARRASSMENT, BUT ALSO TO ACT WITH A LIGHTNESS OF TOUCH AND TO SHARE THE GREAT HUMOR WITH WHICH PATIENTS OFTEN CONFRONT THEIR LOSSES.

DYING INEVITABLY INVOLVES THE DIMINISHMENT OF THE SELF, BUT COM-PASSIONATE CARE CAN HELP TO MAKE IT ALSO A TIME OF GREAT INSIGHT, WHEN PATIENTS FEEL SAFE TO CONFRONT WHAT LIES AT THEIR VERY CORE.

VICTOR PACE

CONSULTANT, ST. CHRISTOPHER'S HOSPICE, UNITED KINGDOM

KINDNESS IS MORE IMPORTANT THAN WISDOM, AND THE RECOGNITION OF THIS IS THE BEGINNING OF WISDOM.

THEODORE ISAAC RUBIN

U.S. PSYCHIATRIST, AUTHOR

KINDNESS IN MIND

THERAPY IS NOT AND NEVER SHOULD BE KIND—IF BY KINDNESS WE MEAN A SYRUPY ELIXIR OF SOPPY SYMPATHY.

TO BE TRULY KIND, A THERAPIST NEEDS PHENOMENAL STRENGTH, ENDURANCE AND GENEROSITY OF SPIRIT. IT MEANS HAVING THE GUTS, HUMILITY AND WISDOM TO FACE ONE'S OWN NIGHTMARISH CRUELTY, RACISM, INDIFFERENCE AND BLINDNESS. IN MY BUSINESS, KINDNESS MEANS BEING ABLE TO SURVIVE VORACIOUS ATTACKS AND INSIDIOUS ASSAULTS FROM PEOPLE WHO ARE HURTING MORE THAN THEY CAN BEAR, AND TO STILL BE THERE PATIENTLY AND FAITHFULLY, HOUR AFTER HOUR, DAY AFTER DAY, MONTH AFTER MONTH AND YEAR AFTER YEAR.

THERAPY DEMANDS A LOVING KINDNESS MADE OF FORMIDABLE RESILIENCE; LISTENING BEYOND WORDS AND THROUGH SILENCE, ALLOWING PATIENTS TO INVADE OUR MINDS, BODIES AND SOULS, TO STRETCH, CHALLENGE AND BEND US WITHOUT BREAKING OUR FAITH.

WITH THIS SORT OF KINDNESS, THERAPY WOULD BE SEEN AS THE BRAVE AND COURAGEOUS ENTERPRISE IT IS. PEOPLE WOULD NOT CALL EACH

OTHER 'MENTAL' OUT OF FEAR AND IGNORANCE, AND WE WOULD NEVER FORGET HOW TERRIFYING IT IS TO FEEL LITTLE, LOST, CRAZY OR ALONE. WE WOULD ALL BE KIND ENOUGH AND WISE ENOUGH TO RECOGNIZE THAT EACH OF US HAS THE INNATE CAPACITY FOR GOOD AND EVIL, CRUELTY AND KINDNESS, AND THERE MIGHT BE TIMES WHEN ALL OF US—THERAPISTS INCLUDED—NEED HELP. THAT HELP MAY TAKE THE FORM OF A SENSITIVE REMARK, A BLUNT COMMENT, OR THE SIMPLE ACT OF LISTENING TO THE UNSPEAKABLE WHEN IT HAS TO BE HEARD, WHEN MERE WORDS ARE MEANINGLESS.

MARILYN MATHEW

JUNGIAN ANALYST, UNITED KINGDOM

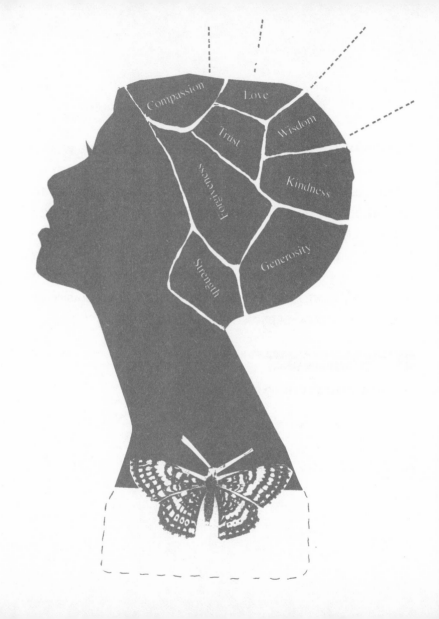

KINDNESS ANTEDATES PSYCHIATRY BY HUNDREDS OF YEARS; ITS ANTIQUITY SHOULD NOT LESSEN YOUR OPINION OF ITS USEFULNESS.

ROSEWELL GALLAGER, M.D.

I SHALL PASS THROUGH THIS WORLD BUT ONCE.
IF, THEREFORE, THERE BE ANY KINDNESS I CAN SHOW, OR ANY
GOOD THING I CAN DO, LET ME DO IT NOW; LET ME NOT DEFER
IT OR NEGLECT IT, FOR I SHALL NOT PASS THIS WAY AGAIN.

ETIENNE DE GRELLET

"LET US
BE KINDER
TO ONE
ANOTHER."

ALDOUS HUXLEY
ON HIS DEATHBED

WHAT WOULD THE WORLD LOOK LIKE IF BUSINESSES WERE REQUIRED TO BE KIND?

.65 53.35 22.56 - 15.3 821 27.65 +.24
.43 42.40 20.19 1.9 25.9 1671 2.91 +.21
.07 36.30 26.94 0.9 20.6 2684 40.76 +.35
1.01 56.99 34.25 2.2 21.8 29445 26.35 ..25
-.03 24.45 15.13 0.4 10.7 10185 33.75 +.33
-2.75 86.20 43.85 0.1 + ♥ 523 19.73 -.08
+.39 49.88 31.04 4.1 78.0 463 39.17 +.06
+.♥ 12.15 6.88 0.9 57.8 6981 19.06 ..2
-.24 37.50 26.31 -1.16 .1 779 6.16
+.53 70.75 37.56 - 36 8.17 +
-.16 13.57 8.60 9.0 42.1 467 6.10 -
-.45 42.50 33.25 2.1 -.21 46793 15.35 -
47.45 29.44 - -.43 11 9.78 +
35 18.04 9.80 .80 14.38 751 61.18
20 +.05 18.75 12 12.9 23.57
12 -.08 31.20 25.60 + ♥ 30.2 23860 11.88
29 -.04 95 70.01 1.3 14.1 12112
3.60 +.93 9 2.2 15.8 2910 37.78
3.77 -.15 21.29 38 2.7 16.7 5617 28.4
17.41 -.29 52.75 17.37 - 13.3 3376 20.7
23.20 -.80 37.88 36 0.9 7.3 648
48.94 -1.04 54.95 20.50 0.2 33.1 10465 33.
28 -.60 35.50 30.06 0.9 4995 31
46.99 +.54 54.52 41.05 1.1 18.3 1286 45
♥ 72.50 18.88 2.5 308

COMPASSIONATE CAPITALISM

THE CULTURE OF 1990S COWBOY CAPITALISM, WITH ITS DEMAND FOR 30 TO 50 PERCENT RETURNS TO SHAREHOLDERS AND ITS OFFER OF TENS OF MILLIONS OF DOLLARS IN STOCK OPTIONS FOR THE CEO'S WHO PRODUCE THEM, NURTURED GREED AND CELEBRATED IT AS A VIRTUE. IT VENERATED THE MOST RUTHLESS AND RAPACIOUS OF CORPORATE EXECUTIVES AND SPED THEIR RISE TO THE PINNACLES OF CORPORATE POWER. KINDNESS WAS CONSIDERED A CHARACTER FLAW TO BE PUNISHED BY EXPULSION AND THE DERISION OF PEERS.

IT IS ENTIRELY WITHIN OUR MEANS TO CREATE LOCAL LIVING ECONOMIES THAT FAVOR ENTERPRISES THAT ARE KIND, LIFE-SERVING, AND ACCOUNTABLE TO COMMUNITY NEEDS AND VALUES—COMPRISED OF HUMAN-SCALE ENTERPRISES OWNED BY LOCAL STAKEHOLDERS WHO ARE PERSONALLY ACCOUNTABLE TO THEIR NEIGHBORS FOR THE CONSEQUENCES OF THEIR ACTIONS. WHEN A FIRM IS OWNED BY WORKERS, COMMUNITY MEMBERS, CUSTOMERS OR SUPPLIERS WHO DIRECTLY BEAR THE CONSEQUENCES OF ITS ACTIONS, IT IS MORE LIKELY TO PROVIDE EMPLOYEES WITH SAFE, MEANINGFUL, FAMILY-WAGE JOBS; CUSTOMERS WITH GOOD SERVICE AND USEFUL, SAFE, QUALITY

PRODUCTS; SUPPLIERS WITH STEADY MARKETS AND FAIR DEALS; AND COMMUNITIES WITH A HEALTHY SOCIAL AND NATURAL ENVIRONMENT.

FORTUNATELY, THE VAST MAJORITY OF THE WORLD'S BUSINESSES ARE HUMAN-SCALE, OWNED BY LOCAL STAKEHOLDERS AND FULLY LIABLE. THEY PROVIDE MOST EMPLOYMENT AND ACCOUNT FOR MOST NEW IDEAS. THEY ARE THE POTENTIAL BUILDING BLOCKS OF NEW ECONOMIES FREED FROM THE CORPORATE PATHOLOGY. OUR PRESENT CHALLENGE IS TO REWRITE THE RULES OF BUSINESS TO FAVOR SUCH ENTERPRISES AND ENCOURAGE THEM TO GROW AMONG THEMSELVES THE WEBS OF RELATIONSHIPS OF A PLANETARY SYSTEM OF LOCAL LIVING ECONOMIES THAT WILL ONE DAY DISPLACE THE SUICIDE ECONOMY AND ITS PATHOLOGICAL INSTITUTIONS.

DAVID KORTEN

PRESIDENT, THE PEOPLE-CENTERED DEVELOPMENT FUND
BOARD CHAIR, THE POSITIVE FUTURES NETWORK

A WOMAN'S PREROGATIVE

KINDNESS SOFTENS THE DEALS. IT OPENS THE DOOR TO MORE HUMAN APPROACHES. TO BE KIND IN A NEGOTIATION CREATES A GREAT ATMOSPHERE; IT IS EVEN FUN TO SEE HOW, THROUGH IT, OTHER PEOPLE'S ATTITUDES CAN BE CHANGED. WHEN A BUSINESS IS BUILT WITH KINDNESS, THE APPROACH AND THE RESULT CAN ONLY BE POSITIVE. KINDNESS IS LINKED TO GOOD INTENTIONS AND A BUSINESS WITH GOOD INTENTIONS BENEFITS EVERYONE INVOLVED.

THERE IS NO NEED TO BEHAVE COLDLY AND WITHOUT FEELING WHEN WE NEGOTIATE. THE BUSINESS WORLD HAS BECOME COLD BECAUSE WE HUMANS CREATED IT THAT WAY. YET I CANNOT IMAGINE A WOMAN WITHOUT KINDNESS. IT WOULD BE LIKE LOSING A STRONG AND BEAUTIFUL ELEMENT THAT IS PART OF HER OWN NATURE, REGARDLESS OF THE

FIELD OR THE ACTIVITY THAT SHE DECIDES TO PERFORM. I DO NOT SEE A DIVORCE BETWEEN BEING A WOMAN AND ANY OTHER TASK. IT IS LIKE CREATING A DISTANCE WITHIN OURSELVES, LIKE DISINTEGRATING OUR OWN ESSENCE.

WE WOMEN HAVE GREAT INFLUENCE, AND WE NEED TO BECOME WARRIORS OF PEACE, GUARDIANS OF LOVE AND AGENTS OF KINDNESS. THE RESULT CAN ONLY BE THE GREAT SATISFACTION OF CREATING HAPPINESS, AND THIS IS CONTAGIOUS.

ADRIANA DE GASPAR DE ALBA

MEXICAN ENTREPRENEUR

KINDNESS, OFF THE RACK

LET'S BE CONCRETE. IF RETAILERS REQUIRED THAT IN THEIR CONTRAC-TORS' FACTORIES THE WORKERS BE TREATED WITH KINDNESS, THEN AT A MINIMUM, THE LEGAL RIGHTS AFFORDED THE WORKERS UNDER LOCAL AND INTERNATIONAL LAW WOULD BE STRICTLY ADHERED TO.

IF THIS WERE THE CASE, YOU WOULD NOT HAVE YOUNG WOMEN IN BANGLADESH FORCED TO WORK 14 TO 15 HOURS A DAY, 7 DAYS A WEEK, 30 DAYS A MONTH, BEING PAID JUST 5 CENTS FOR EVERY $17.99 SHIRT THEY SEW, AND LIVING IN UTTER MISERY. THE WOMEN WOULD NOT BE BEATEN AND DENIED MATERNITY BENEFITS. THE WOMEN WOULD NOT BE SICK AND EXHAUSTED, THEIR FAMILIES COLLAPSING BECAUSE THEY ARE NEVER HOME, THEIR CHILDREN LEFT ALONE. THEY WOULD NOT BE FIRED WHEN THEY REACHED 30 YEARS OF AGE, BECAUSE THE COMPANIES FEEL THE WOMEN ARE WORN OUT AND WANT TO REPLACE THEM WITH ANOTHER CROP OF YOUNG GIRLS. IF THE WORKERS WERE TREATED WITH KINDNESS, THEY WOULD NOT BE ATTACKED, FIRED AND BLACKLISTED WHEN THEY ORGANIZED TO DEFEND THEIR MOST BASIC RIGHTS.

DISNEY AND THE OTHER RETAILERS PERPETUATE A STRUCTURE OF VIOLENCE IN THE GLOBAL ECONOMY. THEY DEMAND ALL SORTS OF

ENFORCEABLE LAWS—INTELLECTUAL PROPERTY AND COPYRIGHT LAWS—BACKED UP BY STIFF PENALTIES TO PROTECT THEIR TRADEMARKS, LOGOS AND ROYALTIES. IF A DAY CARE CENTER SOMEWHERE USES THE IMAGE OF MICKEY MOUSE TO DECORATE ITS PLAYGROUND WALLS WITHOUT PAYING ROYALTIES, DISNEY WILL TRACK IT DOWN AND SUE. BUT WHEN YOU ASK DISNEY, CAN WE NOT ALSO LEGALLY PROTECT THE BASIC RIGHTS OF THE 16-YEAR-OLD WHO SEWED ITS GARMENTS, THE COMPANY RESPONDS BY SAYING: "NO, TO PROTECT HER HUMAN AND WORKER RIGHTS WOULD BE AN IMPEDIMENT TO FREE TRADE." SO, THE TRADEMARK IS PROTECTED, BUT NOT THE HUMAN BEING.

TO BE KIND, BRANDS NEED TO SHOW MORE DEVELOPED EMOTIONS THAN FEAR OR GREED. THEY NEED TO USE THEIR CONSIDERABLE POWER TO CARE FOR THOSE WHO SUBJECT TO THEIR POWER.

CHARLES KERNAGHAN

FOUNDER, THE NATIONAL LABOR COMMITTEE
UNITED STATES

FINANCE THAT DOESN'T
PERPETUATE POVERTY

THE CORE PREMISE OF THE FINANCIAL MODEL THAT NOW RUNS THE
WORLD IS SIMPLE: MONEY IS SMARTER THAN PEOPLE, SO IF RULE-
MAKERS WOULD SIMPLY GRANT FINANCIAL CAPITAL THE RIGHT TO
FLOW FREELY WORLDWIDE, GLOBAL POVERTY WOULD EVAPORATE
LIKE DEWDROPS IN THE MORNING SUN.

IF FINANCE WERE READILY VISIBLE, THAT PREPOSTEROUS PREMISE
WOULD BE EXPOSED AS THE NONSENSE IT OBVIOUSLY IS. TO MAKE
FINANCIAL INSTITUTIONS KIND, WE MUST DEMYSTIFY FINANCE AND
CHRONICLE THE PATTERNS ITS FORCES CREATE. REQUIRED TO BE KIND,
FINANCIAL INSTITUTIONS WOULD FAVOR INCLUSION, AND THEIR
OPERATIONS WOULD BE DESIGNED TO ENSURE THE BROAD-BASED
DISTRIBUTION OF BOTH ASSETS AND INCOME.

FIRMS WOULD BE FINANCED SO THAT A COMPONENT OF THEIR OWN-
ERSHIP BECOMES LOCAL, PERSONALIZED AND HUMAN, SO THAT

FINANCIAL FORCES ARE NO LONGER SO IMPERSONAL AND DUMBED-
DOWN. WITH A STAKE OWNED BY EMPLOYEES, CUSTOMERS AND LOCAL
RESIDENTS. WEALTH WOULD ACCRUE LOCALLY AND REVENUE FLOWS
WOULD IRRIGATE LOCAL ECONOMIES WITH PURCHASING POWER. WITH
KINDER FINANCIAL INSTITUTIONS, THE FORCES OF FINANCE WOULD
OPERATE AS ADAM SMITH ENVISIONED, RESPONDING TO THE
CONCERNS OF PEOPLE.

JEFF GATES

FORMER COUNSEL TO THE U.S. SENATE COMMITTEE ON FINANCE
AUTHOR, *THE OWNERSHIP SOLUTION* AND *DEMOCRACY AT RISK.*
PRESIDENT, THE SHARED CAPITALISM INSTITUTE

KINDNESS OR REVOLUTION

THE UNNECESSARY SUFFERING OF THE OGONI PEOPLE AT THE HANDS OF THE GOVERNMENT AND THE OIL COMPANIES FOR MANY YEARS MIGHT HAVE BEEN AVOIDED WERE KINDNESS A CONDITION OF THE EXISTENCE OF THE GOVERNMENT AND THE OIL COMPANIES.

THE FACT THAT PEOPLE RESPOND POSITIVELY TO LOVE, ACCEPTANCE AND KINDNESS IS NOT JUST A CREATION OF SOCIAL SCIENTISTS. IT'S A FACT OF HUMAN NATURE. THE OGONI PEOPLE ARE A PART OF HUMAN NATURE AND THEY DESERVE LOVE, ACCEPTANCE AND KINDNESS FROM THE GOVERNMENT AND THE OIL COMPANIES. THE BIOLOGICAL, PSYCHOLOGICAL AND SOCIAL FACTORS RESPONSIBLE FOR KINDNESS ARE URGENTLY NEEDED IN OUR SOCIETY TODAY.

WE SHOULD BE WORKING ON MENTAL TRANSFORMATION, WHICH WILL EVENTUALLY LEAD TO INDIVIDUAL TRANSFORMATION. A REVOLU-TION IN KINDNESS CAN CREATE A CORRUPTION-FREE PUBLIC SECTOR. BUT WE MUST BUILD MORAL CAPACITY WITHIN INDIVIDUALS, COMMUNITIES AND SOCIAL INSTITUTIONS. THAT IS WHAT IS LACKING IN NIGERIA TODAY.

LAZARUS TAMANA   **THE OGONI FOUNDATION**

AN INDUSTRY OF KINDLY STRANGERS

WHEN TRAVEL IS UNDERTAKEN WITH AN EYE TO KINDNESS, TOURISTS WILL TRAVEL WITH HUMILITY AND WITH A DESIRE TO LEARN. THEY WILL THINK OF THEMSELVES AS GUESTS IN SOMEBODY ELSE'S HOME. BY TRAVELING WITH RESPECT, THEY WILL EARN RESPECT. IN FACT, TOURISTS WILL "TRAVEL LIKE GANDHI WITH SIMPLE CLOTHES, OPEN EYES AND AN UNCLUTTERED MIND," AS RICK STEVES SAID.

HOLIDAYS WILL BE ABOUT MUTUALLY BENEFICIAL EXCHANGES OF TRUST, WISDOM AND HUMOR WITH LOCAL PEOPLE RATHER THAN ABOUT BEING COCOONED IN COMPOUNDS MARKETED AS ALL INCLU-SIVE RESORTS. HOLIDAY STORIES ABOUT THE DIVERSITY OF LOCAL CULTURES AND ABOUT THE NEW FRIENDS AND KNOWLEDGE THAT VISITORS HAVE GAINED, WILL REPLACE STORIES ABOUT THE CHEAPNESS OF THE RESORT.

INSTEAD OF HAWKING A SUPERFICIAL EXOTICISM AND A RECON-STRUCTED ETHNICITY, THE TOURISM INDUSTRY WILL TREASURE AND CELEBRATE LOCAL CULTURES. RATHER THAN TRINKETIZE THEM, DEGRADE ECOSYSTEMS AND COCA-COLONIZE THE PLANET, THE INDUSTRY WILL SERVE TO ENHANCE AND PROTECT FRAGILE CULTURES AND THE ENVIRONMENTS THAT THEY DEPEND ON.

THE TOURISM INDUSTRY WILL CEASE TO "DISCOVER," EXPLOIT AND DISCARD DESTINATIONS IN ORDER TO MOVE ON TO AND WRECK THE NEXT UNSPOILED PARADISE. RATHER THAN IMPOSING ITS WILL ON DESTINATIONS, THE TRAVEL INDUSTRY WILL WORK IN PARTNERSHIP WITH LOCAL PEOPLE AND GOVERNMENTS TO CREATE BETTER PLACES FOR LOCAL COMMUNITIES AND FOR TOURISTS.

AND WE WILL SEE A REVOLUTION OF UNDERSTANDING BETWEEN PEOPLE FROM DIFFERENT CULTURES. THE CULTURE OF FEAR AND MISTRUST GENERATED BY THE MEDIA WILL BE REPLACED WITH A CULTURE OF UNDERSTANDING AND RESPECT, GENERATED BY SHARED EXPERIENCES. TOURISTS WILL REDISCOVER THE MAGIC OF TRAVEL.

JUSTIN FRANCIS

CO-FOUNDER OF RESPONSIBLETRAVEL.COM

WHAT IF THE MEDIA WERE REQUIRED TO BE KIND?

WHAT IF JOURNALISTS WERE KIND?

THROUGH JOURNALISM WE ENGAGE IN THE LIFE OF OUR COMMUNI-
TIES; ITS FACTS AND STORIES ARE A MEANS TO WISER ENDS, THE BASIS
FOR MAKING JUDGMENTS ABOUT WHO TO VOTE FOR AND WHY IT
MATTERS, WHAT'S FOR DINNER AND WHO, METAPHORICALLY, IS
PICKING UP THE TAB. (ME? GIVEN WHAT I'VE READ, I THINK I'LL HAVE THE
WILD SALMON WITH A SIDE OF ORGANIC GREENS.)

YET THINK ABOUT MUCH OF WHAT WE CALL JOURNALISM TODAY.
MUCH OF 'THE NEWS' LEADS NOWHERE MORE PROFOUND THAN THE
MALL, NOWHERE MORE REAL THAN THE CINEPLEX. THE 6 O'CLOCK
NEWS IS A REALITY-BASED ENTERTAINMENT DEVISED TO TITILLATE
MORE THAN EDUCATE, A CHEAP CONFECTION DESIGNED TO AGGRE-
GATE EYEBALLS FOR ADVERTISERS.

KIND JOURNALISM TAKES A DIFFERENT COURSE. A FEW YEARS AGO A
MOTHER JONES MAGAZINE STAFFER TOLD ME THIS STORY: A PREACHER
RETIRES, RETURNING TO THE COUNTRY TO LIVE IN A COTTAGE ON THE
BANK OF A RIVER. ONE SPRING DAY, SITTING ON HER PORCH AND
WATCHING THE RIVER FLOW BY, SHE HEARS A TERRIFIED VOICE CALLING
FROM THE RIVER. SCANNING THE WATER, SHE SEES A DESPERATE YOUNG
MAN BEING PULLED ALONG BY THE CURRENT, THRASHING, UNABLE TO

SWIM. THE PREACHER REACTS QUICKLY, DIVES INTO THE WATER AND REACHES THE YOUNG MAN IN TIME TO HELP HIM SAFELY TO THE SHORE.

THE NEXT DAY, THE SCENE REPEATS ITSELF—THE PREACHER PULLS A YOUNG WOMAN FROM THE RIVER. THE DAY AFTER, THE PREACHER RESCUES TWO MORE NEAR-VICTIMS. THE NEXT DAY, TWO MORE. BY NOW THE PREACHER'S HAPPINESS AT BEING ABLE TO HELP HAS BEEN REPLACED BY A DEEP ANXIETY: SHE'S EXHAUSTED, AND THE RIVER'S CURRENTS ARE STRONG. SOONER OR LATER, SOMEONE IS SURE TO DROWN. SO THE PREACHER DECIDES TO WALK UPSTREAM—SHE WANTS TO FIND OUT WHO IS PUSHING THE PEOPLE IN.

THAT'S WHAT GREAT JOURNALISTS DO: THEY WALK UPSTREAM—AND REPORT BACK TO THE REST OF US ABOUT WHAT THEY'VE SEEN.

IF MORE JOURNALISTS WERE KIND, LEGIONS WOULD BE TRAMPING UP RIVER TO LOOK FIRST HAND AT THE PROBLEMS OF OUR CITIES, AT THE GAP BETWEEN RICH AND POOR AND WHAT IT MEANS, AT THE IMPACT OF INDUSTRY ON OUR HEALTH AND ENVIRONMENT. TOUGH WORK, BUT KIND JOURNALISM.

JAY HARRIS   **PUBLISHER, *MOTHER JONES* MAGAZINE**

KINDNESS MEANS FACING HARD TRUTHS

SOMEONE ONCE SAID TO ME THAT THE MOST IMPORTANT THING IN LIFE WAS TO BE KIND. THE PROBLEM WAS THAT I KNEW THIS PERSON WOULDN'T BUY A NEWSPAPER AND WOULD CHANGE CHANNELS DURING THE TV NEWS IF THE HEADLINES LOOKED UNPLEASANT— ANYTHING SO AS NOT TO FACE THE FACT THAT SOMETIMES IT'S NOT A PARTICULARLY NICE WORLD WE LIVE IN. YET IT IS ESSENTIAL THAT WE LOOK UGLY, EVIL THINGS IN THE FACE AND NOT TURN AWAY.

SO, KIND IS NOT A WORD THAT I WOULD NECESSARILY USE TO DESCRIBE SELFLESS CONCERN FOR OTHERS, AND THE INEVITABLE PERSONAL DISTRESS THAT ONE CAN FEEL AS A RESULT.

WE LIVE IN A WORLD OBSESSED WITH PACKAGING AND NOT CONTENT. SO MANY OF US DON'T GIVE A DAMN ABOUT THINGS JUST SO LONG AS

THEY LOOK GOOD. WHO CARES WHAT WE DO AS LONG AS NO ONE FINDS OUT WHEN WE DO SOMETHING WRONG?

LOVE, ON THE OTHER HAND, STRIKES ME AS MUCH QUIETER AND MORE PROFOUND, YET MORE DYNAMIC. IT IS ITS OWN REWARD. LOVE EMBRACES KINDNESS. IT'S UNIQUE, LIMITLESS AND UNFATHOMABLE, THE MOST POWERFUL RESOURCE FOR GOOD.

DAVID HIGGS MBE

ENVIRONMENTAL PRESS AGENCY

REPORTING FROM THE HEART

KINDNESS, INSTITUTIONALIZED IN A MEDIA SYSTEM, CAN ONLY EMERGE WHEN HEART-CENTERED INDIVIDUAL REPORTERS ARE ALLOWED TO PURSUE NEWS STORIES THAT ENCOMPASS THEIR NATURAL, INTERNAL-IZED VALUES. NEWS REPORTERS BELIEVE IN FREEDOM OF INFORMATION, THE PUBLIC'S RIGHT TO KNOW, THE FIRST AMENDMENT OF THE U.S. CONSTITUTION, AND IN OUR AMERICAN CULTURAL VALUES OF FREEDOM AND DEMOCRACY.

UNFORTUNATELY, THE BIG CORPORATE MEDIA SYSTEMS TODAY TEND TO LET PROFIT AND POWER DOMINATE POLICY DECISIONS RATHER THAN HUMAN VALUES AND KINDNESS. REPORTERS ARE FACED WITH CAREER SURVIVAL CHOICES AND ARE OBLIGATED TO FOLLOW THE PARTY LINE, REPORTING ENTERTAINMENT NEWS AND GIVING PRIORITY TO THE BOTTOM LINE.

THIS STRUCTURAL ARRANGEMENT IS WHAT MEDIA UNKINDNESS LOOKS LIKE IN AMERICA TODAY. IT IS A SUBTLE SYSTEM OF INFORMATION

SUPPRESSION IN THE NAME OF CORPORATE PROFIT AND SELF INTEREST THAT REFUSES TO SUPPORT HEART-CENTERED REPORTING FOR HUMAN BETTERMENT.

IMAGINE NEWSPAPERS THAT PLACED THE CONCERNS OF THE HOMELESS ON THE FRONT PAGE, EXPOSED THE HIDDEN MOTIVATIONS OF THE BEHIND-THE-SCENES DECISIONMAKERS, AND TREATED HEART-LESSNESS AS A MAJOR CRIME.

OPPORTUNITIES FOR A GRASSROOTS MEDIA BASED ON KINDNESS ARE EMERGING WITH THE GLOBAL MEDIA AND DEMOCRACY MOVEMENTS. INDEPENDENT NEWSPAPERS, MICRORADIO AND THE INDYMEDIA.ORG WEBSITES ARE BUILDING KINDNESS INTO NEWS REPORTING.

PETER PHILLIPS

SOCIOLOGY PROFESSOR, SONOMA STATE UNIVERSITY
DIRECTOR, PROJECT CENSORED

HOW DOES THAT MAKE YOU FEEL?

ONCE, WHEN I WAS A YOUNG JOURNALIST WITH THE *MIAMI DAILY NEWS* IN FLORIDA, I WAS SENT OUT ON A STORY ABOUT A YOUNG KID DROWNING IN ONE OF THE MANY DADE COUNTY CANALS. IT WAS NOT AN UNCOMMON OCCURRENCE AND GENERALLY WARRANTED ONLY A FEW PARAGRAPHS IN THE BACK PAGES. BUT WHILE GETTING INFORMATION FROM THE MOTHER, I DISCOVERED THAT THE BOY WOULD HAVE CELEBRATED HIS EIGHTH BIRTHDAY A WEEK LATER.

I TOLD THE CITY EDITOR WHO THOUGHT IT MIGHT MAKE A GOOD FEATURE. WE DIDN'T DISCUSS THE ETHICS. A WEEK LATER, I GRABBED A PHOTOGRAPHER AND WENT BACK OUT TO SEE THE MOTHER. WHEN SHE OPENED THE DOOR, I SAID: "TODAY WOULD HAVE BEEN ROBERT'S EIGHTH BIRTHDAY. HOW DOES THAT MAKE YOU FEEL?" THE MOTHER BROKE DOWN, THE PHOTOGRAPHER GOT TERRIFIC SHOTS OF THE GRIEVING MOTHER, AND I GOT A FRONT-PAGE BYLINE.

THAT NIGHT I WENT HOME AND I WEPT. WHAT KIND OF MONSTER HAD I TURNED INTO TO GET A FRONT-PAGE STORY? AS IT TURNED OUT, THAT EXPERIENCE WAS ONE OF SEVERAL THAT CAUSED ME TO QUIT JOURNALISM. IF, INSTEAD, I HAD BEEN KIND THAT DAY, I WOULD HAVE RETURNED TO COMFORT THE MOTHER, AND NOT EXPLOIT HER NOR MY READERS. IF JOURNALISTS WERE KIND, THEY WOULD NO LONGER ASK GRIEVING VICTIMS, "HOW DOES THAT MAKE YOU FEEL?" THERE WOULD BE LESS EXPLOITATION AND THE WORLD WOULD BE A LITTLE BIT KINDER.

CARL JENSEN

FOUNDER, PROJECT CENSORED

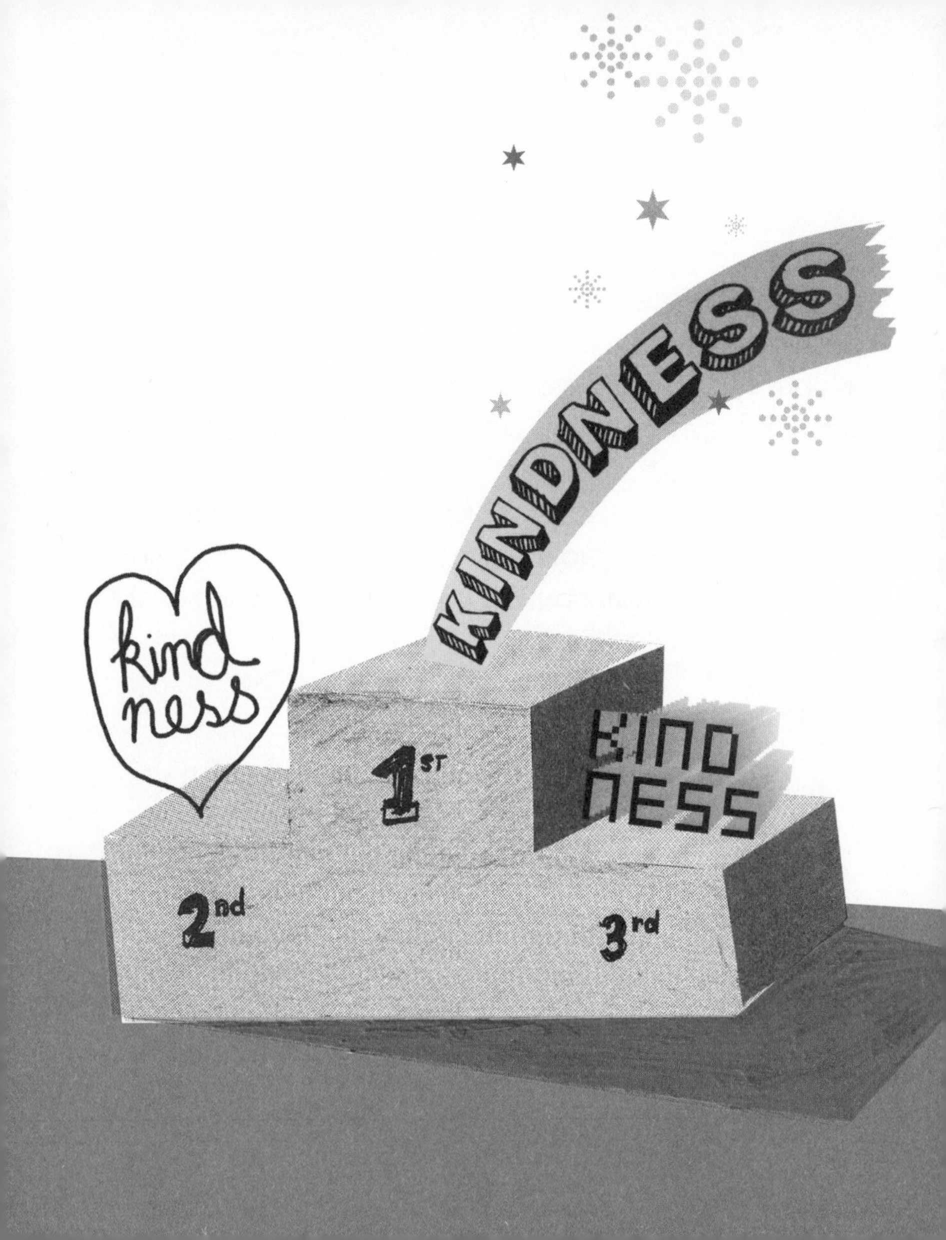
KINDNESS
kind
ness
1ST
KIND
NESS
2nd
3rd

THREE THINGS IN HUMAN LIFE ARE IMPORTANT:
THE FIRST IS TO BE KIND. THE SECOND IS TO BE KIND
AND THE THIRD IS TO BE KIND.

HENRY JAMES

U.S. AUTHOR

WHAT IF POLITICIANS WERE REQUIRED TO BE KIND?

LICENSE FOR LEADERSHIP

IMAGINE A WORLD IN WHICH THOSE WHO CLAIM TO LEAD US MUST FIRST MAKE A PILGRIMAGE TO HIROSHIMA, AUSCHWITZ AND THE KILLING FIELDS OF CAMBODIA, AND PUBLICLY PLEDGE "NEVER AGAIN."

IMAGINE A WORLD IN WHICH LEADERS MUST GO TO BHOPAL AND SAY TO THE VICTIMS: "WE ARE TRULY SORRY. THIS WILL NEVER HAPPEN AGAIN, ANYWHERE."

IMAGINE, TOO, THOSE LEADERS GOING TO PLACES WHERE LOVE, KINDNESS, FORGIVENESS, SACRIFICE, COMPASSION, WISDOM, INGENUITY AND FORESIGHT HAVE BEEN EVIDENT. WHAT MIGHT THEY LEARN FROM ASSISI, THE HOME OF ST. FRANCIS? FROM LE CHAMBON WHERE FRENCH VILLAGERS ACTED TO SAVE JEWS DURING THE NAZI OCCUPATION? FROM A NIGHT IN A HOMELESS SHELTER IN NEW YORK? OR FROM THE RESEARCH CENTER OF LAS GAVIOTAS IN COLOMBIA, WHERE PAOLO LUGARI AND HIS TEAM ARE FORGING A TRULY SUSTAIN-ABLE PATH IN A COUNTRY TORN APART BY GUERRILLA WARFARE AND THE INTERNATIONAL DRUG CARTELS?

IMAGINE A TIME WHEN OUR LEADERS WOULD HAVE TO DESCRIBE PUBLICLY HOW THEY PROPOSED TO CREATE A DECENT AND SUSTAIN-

ABLE PATH OUT OF IMPENDING SOCIAL AND ECOLOGICAL CATASTRO-PHES BEFORE THEY WERE ELECTED. THE SPEECH WOULD NEED TO BE BOTH VISIONARY AND SPECIFIC. THEY COULD HAVE THE PATHOS OF PERICLES' "FUNERAL ORATION," THE KINDNESS OF ST. FRANCIS' "SERMON TO THE BIRDS," THE POWER AND CONCISENESS OF LINCOLN'S "GETTYSBURG ADDRESS," THE QUIET DEFIANCE OF GANDHI'S SPEECH ON NONCOOPERATION, OR THE VISION OF MARTIN LUTHER KING'S "I HAVE A DREAM" SPEECH.

IMAGINE A WORLD IN WHICH THOSE WHO CLAIM TO LEAD US MUST HELP IDENTIFY PLACES AROUND THE WORLD DEGRADED BY HUMAN ACTIONS AND INITIATE THEIR RESTORATION, EVEN IF NO CHANGE WILL BE VISIBLE BY THE TIME THEY ARE UP FOR RE-ELECTION.

YET WE ALSO HAVE TO IMAGINE AND DEMAND A WORLD IN WHICH THOSE WHO LEAD HELP LIFT OUR SIGHTS ABOVE THE CRISES OF THE DAILY HEADLINES AND THE ANNUAL VOTE GRAB TO WHAT COULD BE.

IMAGINE LEADERS WITH MINDS INFORMED THROUGH CONVERSATIONS WITH THE WISEST THINKERS OF OUR TIME. AND BY WISE, WE DO NOT JUST MEAN THOSE WHO ENDORSE A MARKET-LED WORLD.

ODDLY, WE REQUIRE MORE OF PROSPECTIVE CAR DRIVERS THAN WE DO OF OUR LEADERS. THE FORMER MUST AT LEAST PASS A TEST ON THE RULES OF THE ROAD, BUT LEADERS' UNDERSTANDING OF LEADERSHIP IS UNTESTED UNTIL THEY ARE ALREADY IN THE DRIVER'S SEAT. IF ONLY OUR LEADERS WOULD HAVE FIRST TO UNDERSTAND HOW THE WORLD WORKS AS A PHYSICAL SYSTEM, THE POLICIES NECES-SARY FOR SUSTAINABILITY, THE ECONOMICS SUITABLE FOR A SMALL PLANET, THE PRINCIPLES OF ECOLOGICAL DESIGN, AND APPLICABLE TECHNIQUES OF CONFLICT RESOLUTION. IF ONLY OUR LEADERS HAD TO ACTUALLY SPEND TIME LIVING IN HOMELESS SHELTERS, BARRIOS AND REFUGEE CAMPS.

SO TOO, FOR GOOD REASON, DO WE PENALIZE THOSE WHO DRIVE WHEN DRUNK. THE SAME SHOULD BE TRUE OF THOSE INTOXICATED BY EGO, POWER AND IDEOLOGY. WE SHOULD NOT ASK LESS OF OUR LEADERS THAN WE DO OF DRIVERS.

DAVID W ORR

PROFESSOR AND CHAIR, ENVIRONMENTAL STUDIES
OBERLIN COLLEGE

~~GREED~~

~~CONFLICT~~

~~Egoism~~

~~Cynisism~~

~~TYRANNY~~

~~Deception~~

~~Oppression~~

KINDNESS

DAILY DEMOCRACY

IF GOVERNMENTS WERE COMPELLED TO BE KIND, PEOPLE WOULD VIEW GOVERNMENT AS AN INSTRUMENT FOR DOING THE IMPORTANT THINGS THAT PEOPLE CANNOT DO INDIVIDUALLY. CITIZENS WOULD INITIATE WHAT THEY WANT DONE FOR THEIR NEIGHBORHOOD, COMMUNITY, NATION AND WORLD BY SPENDING THEIR TIME, TALENT AND KNOWL-EDGE ENGAGING WITH OTHER CITIZENS IN A DELIBERATIVE PROCESS.

THEY WOULD SELECT THEIR REPRESENTATIVES ON THE BASIS OF MERIT, NOT WHO HAS THE MOST MONEY. BETWEEN ELECTIONS, THEY WOULD PARTICIPATE IN THE MAKING OF POLICY AND IMPLEMENTING PROGRAMS THROUGH THE LEGISLATIVE, EXECUTIVE AND JUDICIAL INSTITUTIONS. WAGING PEACE AND JUSTICE WOULD BE THE PRINCIPAL WAYS GOV-ERNMENT WOULD JUDGE ITS SUCCESSES. GOVERNMENT WOULD ALLOW ITSELF TO BE CHANGED SIMPLY BECAUSE IT IS OF, BY AND FOR THE PEOPLE WHO CONTROL IT, AS THOMAS JEFFERSON ENVISIONED.

DOING WELL BY ITS CHILDREN, FUTURE GENERATIONS WOULD KEEP THE GOVERNMENT OPERATING AT ITS HIGHEST POTENTIAL—SHAPING AND

FORESEEING THE FUTURE, FORESTALLING PRESENT AND FUTURE PERILS, ENDING POVERTY, BUILDING A RESTORATIVE ECONOMY AND ENVIRON-MENT, EDUCATING STUDENTS FOR CIVIC PARTICIPATION AND ENCOUR-AGING THE EMERGENCE OF PUBLIC PHILOSOPHIES.

THAT IS WHAT A KIND GOVERNMENT DOES—IT BRINGS THE BEST OUT IN PEOPLE TO ACCOMPLISH GOOD WORKS, BOTH PUBLIC AND PRIVATE. THE KINDEST GOVERNMENT IS ONE OF AN ACHIEVEMENT-ORIENTED DEMOCRACY, WHICH CITIZENS PUT IN THE TIME TO SUSTAIN DAILY. A DAILY DEMOCRACY REQUIRES DAILY CITIZENSHIP. FREEDOM IS PARTICI-PATION IN POWER IN ORDER TO GENERATE AND APPLY KNOWLEDGE FOR THE BETTERMENT OF HUMAN BEINGS AND THEIR ENVIRONMENT. A KIND GOVERNMENT HERALDS THAT DEFINITION OF FREEDOM.

RALPH NADER

CONSUMER ADVOCATE AND LAWYER
TWO-TIME U.S. PRESIDENTIAL CANDIDATE

PAX POLITICA

IF GOVERNMENTS WERE KIND, THEY'D REALIZE THAT CONFLICTS ARE RESOLVED AND WARS PREVENTED, NOT BY ARMIES, BUT BY ORDINARY PEOPLE.

ORDINARY PEOPLE LIKE KATARINA KRUHONJA, WHO BRAVED DEATH THREATS FROM A WARLORD IN CROATIA TO SET UP A CITIZENS' PEACE CENTER IN OSIJEK. TODAY THE CENTER SENDS PEACE TEAMS INTO TOWNS AND VILLAGES ALL OVER THE COUNTRY TO BRIDGE THE GULFS OF HATRED SEPARATING CROATS AND SERBS.

PEOPLE LIKE ADRIEN TUYAGA IN BURUNDI WHO WORKS TIRELESSLY TO BRING HUTU AND TUTSI YOUTH—MANY OF THEM FORMER PARAMILITARY SOLDIERS—TOGETHER IN SUCCESSFUL ATTEMPTS TO BREAK THE CYCLE OF VIOLENCE THAT BROUGHT CIVIL WAR TO NEIGHBORING RWANDA.

PEOPLE LIKE THE BUSINESSMAN IN EL SALVADOR, FED UP WITH HIS TRUCKS BEING HIGHJACKED AT GUNPOINT, WHO SET UP A GUNS-FOR-FOOD EXCHANGE AND COLLECTED 3,000 WEAPONS IN TWO WEEKS.

IF GOVERNMENTS WERE KIND, THEY WOULD PROVIDE AT LEAST AS MUCH FUNDING FOR PEOPLE DOING THIS WORK AS THEY DO FOR THE MILITARY. AT THE MOMENT, THE BRITISH GOVERNMENT ALLOCATES 29 BILLION POUNDS PER YEAR FOR THE MILITARY, AND 110 MILLION POUNDS PER YEAR FOR CONFLICT PREVENTION AND CONFLICT RESOLUTION. YET THIS IS BETTER THAN WITH MOST GOVERNMENTS.

KINDNESS IN GOVERNMENT NEEDS TO BE SYNONYMOUS WITH WISDOM. IN ALL CONFLICTS, JUST AS THERE ARE THOSE WHO ARE READY TO PICK UP A GUN, THERE ARE ALSO THOSE WHO WANT TO PREVENT BLOODSHED AND RESOLVE THE ISSUES WITHOUT VIOLENCE. WISDOM LIES IN SUPPORTING SUCH PEOPLE.

SCILLA ELWORTHY

DIRECTOR, THE OXFORD RESEARCH GROUP

THE TRANSFORMATIVE POWER OF KINDNESS

WHEN KINDNESS IS THE ABILITY TO PUT OURSELVES IN SOMEONE ELSE'S PLACE AND TAKE DECISIONS IN CONSEQUENCE, IT GIVES US AUTHORITY AND MAKES VIOLENCE UNNECESSARY. IF WE COULD REPLACE VIOLENT AND UNFAIR GOVERNMENTS WITH KINDLY ONES, PEACE WOULD BE A REALITY AND ALL HUMAN RIGHTS WOULD PREVAIL. HUMANITY NEEDS KIND PEOPLE AT ALL LEVELS MAKING DECISIONS ON INTERNATIONAL AND FINANCIAL AFFAIRS.

MARIS JOSE LUBERTINO

ARGENTINE WOMEN'S HUMAN RIGHTS DEFENDER, LAWYER, PROFESSOR, POLITICIAN AND JOURNALIST

KINDNESS IN CONFLICT

SOME WOULD ARGUE THAT WHEN CONFLICT ENSUES, THE TIME FOR KINDNESS HAS PASSED. DOES THIS MEAN THAT CONFLICT CANNOT, BY DEFINITION, BE KIND? PERHAPS, BUT HOW ABOUT KINDNESS ON AN INDIVIDUAL LEVEL? AS A SOLDIER, YOU ARE TAUGHT THAT KINDNESS TO THE ENEMY IS A WEAKNESS THAT CAN COST YOU OR YOUR FELLOW SOLDIERS THEIR LIVES, YET STILL, EXAMPLES OF KINDNESS IN CONFLICT ABOUND.

THE IMAGE OF THE KNIGHT-LIKE WARRIOR WITH A HIGH SENSE OF HONOR AND CHIVALRY, A PERSON WHO IS CAPABLE OF VIOLENCE BUT WHO PREFERS PEACE AND COMPASSION, IS THE EMBODIMENT OF THIS IDEAL. IT IS SAID THAT NO ONE DESIRES PEACE MORE THAN A SOLDIER, FOR HE HAS THE MOST TO LOSE IN A CONFLICT.

IF MORE POLITICIANS AND DIPLOMATS WERE FORCED TO FIGHT IN THE WARS THEY CAUSED, OR FAILED TO AVOID, MY GUESS IS THAT THERE WOULD BE A LOT LESS OF THEM. AS LONG AS THE PEOPLE WHO START WARS ARE NOT THE ONES WHO MUST FACE DEATH TO FIGHT THEM, OUR BEST HOPE FOR KINDNESS IN CONFLICT LIES IN THE HUMANITY OF THE MEN AND WOMEN ON THE BATTLEFIELD WHO MUST FACE THE ENEMY AND DEATH WITH COURAGE AND COMPASSION.

WARREN PUCKETT

FORMER OFFICER, U.S. ARMY SPECIAL FORCES COMMAND

AN EYE CAN THREATEN LIKE A LOADED AND LEVELED GUN, OR IT CAN INSULT LIKE HISSING OR KICKING; OR, IN ITS ALTERED MOOD, BY BEAMS OF KINDNESS, IT CAN MAKE THE HEART DANCE FOR JOY.

RALPH WALDO EMERSON

U.S. PHILOSOPHER, POET, ESSAYIST

KINDNESS IN THE TRENCHES

KINDNESS IS NOT A WORD THAT USUALLY SPRINGS TO MIND WHEN ONE THINKS OF THE MILITARY. OH SURE, OCCASIONALLY ONE SEES PEOPLE IN UNIFORM FEEDING REFUGEES OR BATTLING RISING FLOOD WATERS, BUT GENERALLY MILITARIES EXIST TO FIGHT, OR BY THREAT OF OVERWHELM-ING FORCE, TO DETER WARS.

IN MOST MILITARY ESTABLISHMENTS, WHILE COURTESY AND GOOD MANNERS ARE EXPECTED AND EVEN DEMANDED WITHIN THE GROUP, PERSONAL KINDNESS TOWARD THE UNIFORMED FOE OR EVEN ENEMY CIVILIANS IS PERCEIVED AS WEAKNESS. THE GOOD SOLDIER IS A TOUGH GUY WHO IS WILLING TO KILL OR BE KILLED, TO DO WHATEVER IS NECESSARY, ACCORDING TO THE ORDERS OF THE DAY. THIS IS NOT TO SAY THAT INDIVIDUAL SOLDIERS DO NOT HAVE NORMAL FEELINGS OF CONCERN AND EMPATHY. THEY ARE HUMAN BEINGS AND, AS SUCH, ARE THE SAME AS YOU AND ME. THERE IS JUST NO PREMIUM ON KINDNESS AS A MILITARY VIRTUE.

WHAT IS NEEDED IS A NEW REALIZATION THAT KINDNESS AND FAIR PLAY, EVEN IN WARFARE, ARE VALUES THAT CAN HELP TO ACHIEVE THE ONLY

JUST OBJECTIVE OF WAR: LASTING AND STABLE PEACE WITH ONE'S ADVERSARIES. EXCESSIVE BRUTALITY AND GRATUITOUS CRUELTY ONLY CREATE NEW GENERATIONS OF ENEMIES AND PROVIDE JUSTIFICATION FOR THE NEXT WAR.

PROPHETS AND THEOLOGIANS OF ALL THE GREAT RELIGIONS HAVE RECOGNIZED THIS FOR CENTURIES, BUT THE MESSAGE IS ALMOST ALWAYS DILUTED BY THOSE SEEKING NATIONAL SECURITY, LEBEN-SRAUM, ETHNIC PURITY, RELIGIOUS HOMOGENEITY OR ANY NUMBER OF OTHER ENDS. UNTIL KINDNESS AND LOVE FOR ONE'S FELLOW HUMAN BEINGS IS RECOGNIZED AS A VIRTUE TO BE CULTIVATED AMONG SOLDIERS AND THE POLICYMAKERS WHO SEND THEM TO WAR, THERE WILL NEVER BE AN END TO WARS?

WILLIAM STUEBNER

EXECUTIVE DIRECTOR, THE INSTITUTE FOR INTERNATIONAL CRIMINAL INVESTIGATIONS

KINDNESS BEGETS KINDNESS

SOPHOCLES GOT IT RIGHT WHEN HE WROTE, "KINDNESS IS THE BEGETTER OF KINDNESS." SHAME HE'S NOT AROUND TODAY AND ABLE TO GO AND EXPLAIN THIS TO THE ISRAELI AND PALESTINIAN AND VARIOUS OTHER WORLD LEADERS WHO DON'T SEEM TO BE ABLE TO UNDERSTAND THAT HATE BEGETS HATE AND GREED BEGETS GREED.

WAYNE HEMINGWAY

FASHION DESIGNER

WHAT WOULD THE WORLD LOOK LIKE IF THE CRIMINAL JUSTICE SYSTEM WERE KIND?

JUSTICE FOR ALL

IF THE CRIMINAL JUSTICE SYSTEM WERE REQUIRED TO BE KIND, MAYBE IT WOULD LOOK SOMETHING LIKE THIS: POLICE OFFICERS WOULD APPROACH ALL CHILDREN AS IF THEY WERE THEIR OWN. THEY WOULD NEVER SLAM KIDS' FACES ONTO CAR HOODS. THEY WOULD LISTEN TO PEOPLE WITH ACCENTS, PEOPLE OF OTHER RACES. THEY WOULD NOT BE PREJUDICED. THEY WOULD NOT HAVE GUNS. PROSECUTORS WOULD DROP CHARGES WHEN THERE WAS INSUFFICIENT EVIDENCE. THEY WOULD NOT BUILD CASES AGAINST INNOCENT PEOPLE FOR POLITICAL REASONS. JUDGES WOULD NOT BE REQUIRED TO USE MANDATORY SENTENCING LAWS. NONVIOLENT DRUG OFFENDERS WOULD BE SENT TO TREATMENT CENTERS, NOT PRISONS. CRIME VICTIMS WOULD BE ABLE TO TALK TO THE PEOPLE WHO VICTIMIZED THEM. THERE WOULD BE NO DEATH PENALTY.

THERE WOULD BE TREATMENT FACILITIES AND THERAPY FOR PRISONERS WHO NEEDED THEM. PRISONERS WOULD LIVE WITH THEIR HUMANITY INTACT. THEY WOULD BE SAFE FROM HARM. THEY COULD PRACTICE THEIR SPIRITUAL BELIEFS WITHOUT HARASSMENT. THEY COULD HAVE CONJUGAL VISITS WITH SPOUSES, ACCESS TO BOOKS, GOOD HEALTH CARE. CALLS TO THEIR LOVED ONES WOULD BE FREE.

HEALING CAN'T HAPPEN IN ISOLATION. COMMUNITIES WOULD BE INVOLVED IN THE PROCESS. VICTIMS WOULD NOT BE FORGOTTEN. VICTIMS OF RAPE, DOMESTIC ABUSE, ROBBERY, ASSAULT, KIDNAPPING AND OTHER CRIMES—AS WELL AS FAMILIES OF VICTIMS—WOULD NOT BE PUSHED ASIDE, IGNORED, ACCUSED, THREATENED, INTIMIDATED, SCARED OR MADE FEARFUL FOR THEIR LIVES. AN INFRASTRUCTURE WOULD BE IN PLACE TO ALLOW THEM TO BE HEARD AND TO BE SAFE.

JUSTICE WOULD BE BLIND. PEOPLE OF COLOR WOULD NOT BE SUSPECTED, ARRESTED, AND SENTENCED BASED ON THEIR RACE. POOR PEOPLE WOULD HAVE THE SAME LEGAL REPRESENTATION AS THE WEALTHY.

IF THE JUSTICE SYSTEM WERE REQUIRED TO BE KIND, IT WOULD BE TOLERANT, UNDERSTANDING, FORGIVING, PEACEFUL AND HELPFUL. LET US EMPATHIZE WITH THOSE WHO ARE DIFFERENT THAN WE ARE. LET US UNDERSTAND THAT POVERTY, RACISM, UNEMPLOYMENT, LACK OF EDUCATION, DRUG ADDICTION, INADEQUATE HOUSING, HUNGER AND ISOLATION CONTRIBUTE TO CRIMINAL BEHAVIOR. LET US BE COMPAS-SIONATE ENOUGH TO BELIEVE THAT PEOPLE CHANGE.

LESLIE GEORGE **JOURNALIST**

CAN JUSTICE BE KIND?

I FIND IT DIFFICULT EVEN TO IMAGINE A CRIMINAL JUSTICE SYSTEM INFUSED WITH KINDNESS. THE UNITED STATES STANDS IN THE MIDST OF A DECADES-LONG EXPANSION OF AN EVER-MEANER PRISON-INDUSTRIAL COMPLEX. THE SYSTEM NOW HOLDS 2 MILLION SOULS, OF WHOM SEVERAL THOUSAND AWAIT EXECUTION AND MANY THOUSANDS MORE ARE HELD FOR YEARS AT A STRETCH IN SENSORY-DEPRIVATION-STYLE SOLITARY CONFINEMENT.

AS IF TO HIGHLIGHT THE VENOMOUS NATURE OF THIS EXPERIMENT, AMERICAN CRIMINAL LAWS WERE LONG AGO REWRITTEN TO EXCISE ANACHRONISTIC REFERENCES TO REHABILITATION AS A PRIMARY GOAL OF IMPRISONMENT. AS THEY ARE NOW WRITTEN, THE LAWS SPEAK ONLY OF PUNISHMENT AND 'DETERRENCE'—WHICH IS A FANCY TERM FOR USING PRISONERS AND THE BRUTAL TREATMENT TO WHICH THEY ARE SUBJECTED AS EXAMPLES TO POTENTIAL LAWBREAKERS.

IF THERE IS A NEXUS BETWEEN THE CRIMINAL JUSTICE SYSTEM AND KINDNESS, IT IS NOT TO BE FOUND AMONG THE VENAL POLITICIANS WHO HAVE BUILT THE SYSTEM OR THE PETTY BUREAUCRATS WHO ADMINISTER IT. RATHER, IT IS TO BE FOUND AMONG THOSE WHO

STRUGGLE AGAINST THE SYSTEM, FROM BOTH WITHIN AND WITHOUT PRISON WALLS. DURING THE YEARS I HAVE SPENT AS A CRIMINAL DEFENSE LAWYER—AND BEFORE THAT AS AN ANTI-PRISON ACTIVIST—I HAVE FOUND MYSELF WORKING WITH SOME OF THE FINEST AND KINDEST PEOPLE I HAVE EVER ENCOUNTERED.

I HAVE KNOWN DEDICATED VOLUNTEER ACTIVISTS WHO HAVE BUILT SOPHISTICATED GRASSROOTS CAMPAIGNS THAT SEEK TO EXPOSE TORTURE AND INJUSTICE. I HAVE KNOWN WOMEN IN PRISON WHO RISK AND SOME-TIMES SUFFER PUNISHMENT FOR SMUGGLING FRESH FRUITS AND VEGETA-BLES—CONTRABAND, ACCORDING TO THE RULES—TO FELLOW PRISONERS BEDRIDDEN WITH AIDS OR CANCER. I HAVE KNOWN LAWYERS WHO HAVE SPENT 10, 20, OR MORE YEARS, OFTEN FOR NO PAY, FIGHTING TO FREE A SINGLE INNOCENT PERSON. AND I HAVE KNOWN PEOPLE OF MEAGER MEANS WHO MANAGE TO SEND 20 DOLLARS EVERY MONTH SO THAT A PRISONER CAN BUY EXTRA FOOD OR WRITING PAPER FROM THE CANTEEN.

I WOULD LIKE SOME DAY TO LIVE IN A SOCIETY WHERE PRISONS ARE UNNECESSARY. IN THE SHORTER TERM, IF OUR CURRENT CRIMINAL JUSTICE SYSTEM IS SOMEHOW TO BE REFORMED, THE TASK WILL NOT BE

ACCOMPLISHED BASED ON THE CRUEL VALUES OF THOSE WHO HAVE BUILT IT, BUT ON THE VALUES OF KINDNESS AND LOVE EXEMPLIFIED BY THOSE WHO REFUSE TO ACCEPT IT AS IT CURRENTLY EXISTS.

SCOTT FLEMING

CRIMINAL DEFENSE LAWYER FROM OAKLAND, CALIFORNIA REPRESENTING HERMAN WALLACE AND ALBERT WOODFOX OF THE ANGOLA 3

THE CHESS TOURNAMENT

I HAVE BEEN IN PRISON FOR 35 YEARS. PRISON IS THE ONLY PLACE I KNOW OF WHERE INDIVIDUALS ARE HIRED, TRAINED AND PAID TO MENTALLY AND PHYSICALLY ABUSE OTHERS. PRISONS, BY THEIR DESIGN, OBLITERATE KINDNESS.

I AM CURRENTLY SPENDING 6 MONTHS IN THE PENITENTIARY'S SUPER-MAXIMUM SECURITY PUNISHMENT CAMP, WHERE WE ARE LOCKED IN OUR CELLS FOR 23 OR 24 HOURS EVERY DAY AND HAVE ALMOST NO PRIVILEGES. THE CONDITIONS HERE ARE ENGINEERED TO BREAK MEN'S WILL. SOME MEN ARE HERE BECAUSE THEY, LIKE ME, HAVE BEEN LABELED REBELLIOUS FOR CHALLENGING THE INHUMANITY OF OUR CONFINEMENT. OTHERS ARE HERE BECAUSE THEY ARE TRULY EMOTION-ALLY AND MENTALLY DAMAGED. THEY DO ACT OUT AND BREAK RULES, BUT THE CONDITIONS HERE SERVE ONLY TO DRIVE THEM FURTHER INTO MADNESS.

WHEN I FIRST ARRIVED AT THIS UNIT, THE MEN WERE CONSTANTLY VERBALLY AND PHYSICALLY ATTACKING EACH OTHER, A RESPONSE TO THE COMPLETE LACK OF KINDNESS IN OUR SURROUNDINGS. MOST MEN

HAVE NO FAMILY OR FRIENDS TO WRITE OR VISIT THEM. THEY TAKE OUT THEIR FRUSTRATION ON EACH OTHER BECAUSE THEY HAVE NO CONTROL OVER THEIR OWN LIVES.

I HAVE ALWAYS TRIED TO HELP THEM OVERCOME THEIR DESTRUCTIVE BEHAVIOR BY BRINGING THEM TOGETHER AND MAKING THEM REALIZE THAT BEING KIND TO ONE ANOTHER IS THE BEST SOLUTION TO MAKING ALL OUR LIVES MORE TOLERABLE. I SET UP A CHESS TOURNAMENT, MAKING THE PRIZE TEN 34-CENT STAMPS—WINNER TAKE ALL. OF COURSE, EVERYONE PARTICIPATED. IT WAS A CLEAR SHOT AT INSTANT WEALTH—FOR MEN WITH NO INCOME, $3.40 CAN BUY A LOT OF POTATO CHIPS FROM THE CANTEEN.

EACH MAN MADE A CHESSBOARD AND CONSTRUCTED PIECES WITH SCRAPS OF PAPER. AS EACH PAIR SHOUTED THEIR MOVES TO ONE ANOTHER, ALL THE OTHER MEN FOLLOWED THE GAMES ON THE BOARDS IN THEIR CELLS. BY THE END OF THE TOURNAMENT, MEN WHO HAD BEEN HOSTILE TO ONE ANOTHER WERE TALKING, AND SO BEGAN A MORE PLEASANT RELATIONSHIP FOR EVERYONE IN THE UNIT.

INVOLVING EVERYONE IN SOME FRIENDLY COMPETITION—AND SHOWING THEM KINDNESS—ALTERED A LOT OF NEGATIVE BEHAVIOR AND ALLOWED EVERYONE TO LIVE IN A MORE HARMONIOUS ENVIRON-MENT. TWO MONTHS INTO MY 6-MONTH SENTENCE HERE, PRACTICALLY ALL OF THE MEN ARE NOW FRIENDS, SHARING AND HELPING EACH OTHER TO EXCEL.

HERMAN WALLACE

POLITICAL PRISONER, ANGOLA, LOUISIANA

THE DEBT OF KINDNESS

I HAVE BEEN IN PRISON FOR OVER 30 YEARS. INTELLECTUALLY, I UNDERSTAND THAT KINDNESS IS SELFLESSNESS. BUT I LIVE IN AN ENVIRONMENT WHERE EVERY DECISION I MAKE CAN BE LIFE-THREATENING.

I HAVE ALWAYS HAD TO RESERVE KINDNESS FOR A SELECT FEW WHO I FEEL SAFE CALLING FRIENDS. BEYOND THOSE SELECT FEW, I MUST QUESTION EVERY ACT TOWARD ME, EVEN THOSE YOU COULD CALL ACTS OF KINDNESS. IN PRISON, EVERY ACT BY ONE HUMAN BEING TOWARD ANOTHER HAS STRINGS ATTACHED. EVEN THOUGH I DO NOT SMOKE, I ALWAYS KEEP SOME TOBACCO IN MY CELL SO THAT I CAN REPAY ANY GIFT THAT IS OFFERED TO ME. I CANNOT ALLOW MYSELF TO OWE ANYTHING TO ANYONE. TO PROTECT MYSELF, I MUST REFUSE OR REJECT ACTS THAT COULD BE CALLED KINDNESS. THIS IS A TERRIBLE WAY FOR A HUMAN BEING TO LIVE.

EVERY TIME I HAVE HAD TO TURN AWAY AN ACT OF KINDNESS, A SMALL PART OF MY SOUL WAS LOST. IT HAS NEVER BEEN AN EASY CHOICE TO MAKE, BUT THESE CHOICES HAVE MADE IT POSSIBLE FOR ME TO HOLD ONTO MY SANITY, SENSE OF SELF-WORTH, AND THE REVOLUTIONARY PRINCIPLES THAT HAVE BEEN MY SOURCE OF STRENGTH.

THAT IS NOT TO SAY THAT I CAN NEVER EXPERIENCE KINDNESS. WITH A SMALL GROUP OF PRISONERS I TRUST ENOUGH TO CALL FRIENDS, I HAVE SHARED KINDNESS OF A TYPE MOST PEOPLE ARE RARELY LUCKY ENOUGH TO EXPERIENCE. WE HAVE BEEN IMPRISONED TOGETHER FOR DECADES, AND THERE IS NOTHING THAT WE WOULD NOT DO FOR OR SHARE WITH ONE ANOTHER. WE HAVE STRUGGLED TOGETHER, BEEN BEATEN TOGETHER, AND SHARED WITH EACH OTHER THE BIRTHS AND DEATHS OF LOVED ONES ON THE OUTSIDE THAT WE HAVE BEEN FORBIDDEN FROM EXPERIENCING FIRST HAND.

I ALSO RECEIVE TREMENDOUS KINDNESS FROM SUPPORTERS ON THE OUTSIDE, SOME OF WHOM ARE STRANGERS. EVERY TIME SOMEONE CARRIES A BANNER CALLING FOR MY FREEDOM, SITS DOWN TO WRITE ME A LETTER, OR TAKES THE TIME TO ATTEND ONE OF MY COURT PROCEEDINGS, IT IS AN ACT OF KINDNESS.

EVERY ACT OF KINDNESS, BY AN INDIVIDUAL OR BY THOUSANDS, IS A POWERFUL TOOL FOR JUSTICE AND FREEDOM.

ALBERT WOODFOX

POLITICAL PRISONER, ANGOLA, LOUISIANA

WHAT IF THE MUSIC INDUSTRY WERE KIND?

PERFECT HARMONY

IF THE MUSIC INDUSTRY WERE KIND, ARTISTS WOULD BE SEEN AS HUMAN BEINGS, NOT PRODUCTS. CREATIVITY WOULD BE WORSHIPPED OVER MONEY. CHARACTER, ABILITY AND ORIGINALITY WOULD BE HONORED OVER AGE, SKIN COLOR AND SEX APPEAL.

LABELS AND MANAGERS WOULD NURTURE AND GUIDE ARTIST DEVELOP-MENT FOR THE LONG-TERM. THOUGHTFUL AND WISE BUDGETING WOULD REPLACE EXTRAVAGANT 'MAKE OR BREAK' CAMPAIGNS WITH COMMITTED, SLOW-BUILD SUSTAINABLE MARKETING STRATEGIES. IN A KIND MUSIC INDUSTRY, BANDS WOULD NEVER BE ABANDONED AFTER ONE 'STIFF' RECORD. THE ARTISTIC TEMPERAMENT WOULD BE UNDERSTOOD AND SUPPORTED FOR ITS EMOTIONAL SENSITIVITY. HEALTH AND WELL-BEING WOULD BE PRIORITIZED OVER GRUELING PROMOTIONAL SCHEDULES.

COMPANIES WOULD NOT ASSUME THAT AGE DICTATES CAREER SPAN.

MUSIC WOULD BE RESPECTED AND CHERISHED AS ONE OF LIFE'S GREATEST GIFTS: A REFLECTION OF OUR UNIQUE CREATIVE POTENTIAL AND RIGHT TO SELF-EXPRESSION.

MISTY OLDLAND **SINGER-SONGWRITER**

MORE LENNON, LESS BRITNEY

IF KINDNESS MATTERED IN THIS INDUSTRY, I DO BELIEVE MUSIC WOULD BE MORE INSPIRING, AS IT IS MEANT TO BE. ARTISTS' MOTIVATION WOULD BE TO MOVE AND INSPIRE PEOPLE RATHER THAN TO GET A GOLD RECORD OR A MUTI-MILLION DOLLAR CONTRACT. IF THE MUSIC INDUSTRY VALUED KINDNESS, I THINK WE WOULD HAVE MORE MUSICIANS LIKE JOHN LENNON AND JONI MITCHELL, AND LESS "AMERICAN IDOL."

TINA SCHLIESKE

MUSICIAN AND RECORDING ARTIST

TINA AND THE B-SIDES

IF HUMANITY MATTERED MORE THAN PROFIT IN THE MUSIC INDUSTRY

I DON'T THINK PROFIT PER SE IS SUCH A BAD THING. WE DO NEED SOME-THING TO MOTIVATE US THAT IS QUANTIFIABLE. BUT WHEN THE INDUSTRY IS IN THE HANDS OF A NARROW GROUP OF PEOPLE (CURRENTLY WHITE MEN), USING MONEY TO QUANTIFY SUCCESS OR TO MEASURE MARKET RESPONSE CAN BE A DANGEROUS THING.

IF HUMANITY OR KINDNESS WERE INCLUDED AS A GOAL, THE MUSIC WOULD JUST BE MORE DIVERSE. POLITICAL PERFORMERS, PEOPLE WHO DON'T MEET A POPULAR STANDARD OF BEAUTY, NON-SUBMISSIVE WOMEN, AND OTHERS WOULD ACTUALLY HAVE A CHANCE. WITHOUT MONEY RUNNING THE SHOW, THE MARKET-DRIVEN SEGREGATION OF MUSIC INTO TIDY, BORING DEMOGRAPHICS WOULD CEASE.

AMY RAY

MUSICIAN AND ACTIVIST, INDIGO GIRLS

VIVE LA DIFFERENCE

IF KINDNESS WERE A PRIORITY, POPULAR MUSIC WOULD BE PROGRES-
SIVE AND ECLECTIC RATHER THAN SAFE AND HOMOGENOUS. RADIO
WOULD BE INTERESTING! PROFIT MOTIVATION DRIVES RECORD
COMPANIES TO SIGN AND PROMOTE SIMILAR SOUNDING ARTISTS IN
HOPES OF CASHING IN ON TRENDS. ONCE THOSE ARTISTS CAN NO
LONGER PRODUCE HITS OF THE CURRENT ILK, THEY ARE DUMPED. IF
KINDNESS AND HUMANITY MOTIVATED THE INDUSTRY, WE WOULD SEE
BANDS AND ARTISTS WITH LONG AND FRUITFUL CAREERS, UNFETTERED
BY THE PRESSURE TO PRODUCE HITS, AND ENCOURAGED, PROMOTED
AND VALUED FOR THE QUALITY AND EXPANSE OF THEIR WORK. WHEN
RECORD COMPANIES GO FOR THE SURE, HUGE HIT, THEY PERPETUATE
FORMULAIC POP AND DISREGARD A WEALTH OF ARTISTS WHOSE MUSIC
WOULD COLLECTIVELY REPRESENT A DIVERSE AND INTERESTING
SPECTRUM OF MUSIC. RECORD COMPANIES AND RADIO PROGRAMMERS
NOTORIOUSLY UNDERESTIMATE THE PALATE OF THE LISTENING AND
BUYING PUBLIC.

EMILY SALIERS

MUSICIAN AND ACTIVIST, INDIGO GIRLS

FEEL INGSk

KINDNESS IN WORDS CREATES CONFIDENCE.

KINDNESS IN THINKING CREATES PROFOUNDNESS.

KINDNESS IN GIVING CREATES LOVE.

LAO-TZU

WHAT WOULD THE WORLD LOOK LIKE IF RELIGION WERE KIND?

RELIGION OF THE HUMAN HEART

A KIND RELIGIOUS WORLD—NOW THERE LIES A RADICAL IDEA. CAN WE IMAGINE A WORLD WHERE JEWS AND MUSLIMS ARE NOT FIGHTING OVER A HOLY LAND THAT SUPPOSEDLY WAS LEFT EXCLUSIVELY TO EACH BY A CONFUSED GOD WHO IS THE GOD OF BOTH?

CAN WE IMAGINE A WORLD WHERE HINDUS AND MUSLIMS ARE NOT KILLING EACH OTHER IN INDIA AND PAKISTAN AND KASHMIR? A WORLD WHERE JERRY FALWELL AND COMPANY ARE NOT CALLING HELL AND DAMNATION DOWN ONTO HOMOSEXUALS AND OTHERS MADE IN THE IMAGE OF GOD? AND WHERE INQUISITIONS AND CRUSADES ARE OUTLAWED AND APOLOGIES ARE MADE BY POPES FOR ANTISEMITISM, WITCH BURNINGS, CRUSADES, AND INQUISITIONS OF THE PAST? AND WHERE THE GOLD STOLEN FROM THE INDIGENOUS PEOPLES OF THE AMERICAS THAT STILL ADORNS THE CHURCHES IN ROME MIGHT BE RETURNED TO ITS POVERTY-STRICKEN RIGHTFUL OWNERS? YES, A KIND RELIGION WOULD BE A REVOLUTION.

THE WORD KINDNESS, AFTER ALL, COMES FROM THE WORD FOR KIN. IT IS ABOUT HOW WE TREAT THOSE WHO ARE NEAREST US. IT IS A FAMILY WORD. IF RELIGION WERE REQUIRED TO BE KIND IT WOULD HAVE TO

FIND KINSHIP WITH OTHER RELIGIONS, OR BETTER STILL, OTHER SPIRITUAL TRADITIONS.

A RECONSTRUCTION OF RELIGION ON THE BASIS OF FIERCE KINDNESS AND REAL KINSHIP WOULD REQUIRE A DECONSTRUCTION AS WELL. ARE WE CAPABLE OF DECONSTRUCTING OUR RELIGIOUS ATTITUDES TO MAKE ROOM FOR THIS RECONSTRUCTIVE KINDNESS TO EMERGE? I WOULD HOPE SO, AND I SUSPECT THAT JESUS AND ISAIAH, BUDDHA AND MUHAMMAD, MARTIN LUTHER KING, JR. AND THE DALAI LAMA WOULD CONCUR. IN FACT, IS IT SO STRANGE A SUGGESTION TO PROPOSE THAT THIS IS WHAT THEY TAUGHT IN THEIR LIFETIMES?

MATTHEW FOX

SPIRITUAL THEOLOGIAN, FOUNDER AND PRESIDENT,
UNIVERSITY OF CREATION SPIRITUALITY, OAKLAND, CALIFORNIA

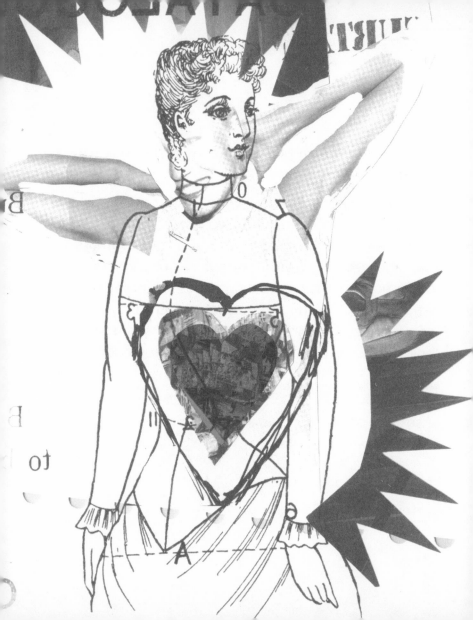

SELFLESS REFLECTION

THE PROPHET BY KAHLIL GIBRAN IS ABOUT KINDNESS THAT GAZES UPON ITSELF IN A MIRROR AND TURNS TO STONE. TRUE KINDNESS HAS TO BE TOTALLY FREE FROM ANY SELF-CONCERN OR SELF REFERENCING. KINDNESS IS GIVING, AND THERE IS NOTHING IN IT FOR THE GIVER EXCEPT THE JOY OF GIVING ITSELF. IF WE LOOK TO SEE OURSELVES IN OUR ACTS OF KINDNESS THEN WHO ARE WE REALLY SERVING?

I LOVE THIS IDEA BECAUSE IN A FEW WORDS IT CONVEYS THAT THERE IS NOTHING MEEK OR MILD ABOUT KINDNESS, THAT IT'S REAL POWER LIES IN RESPONDING TO ITS RELENTLESS DEMAND TO GIVE AND HOLD NOTHING BACK, AND THAT IN ITSELF IS INSPIRING.

LINUS ROACHE

BRITISH ACTOR

TRUE KINDNESS PRESUPPOSES THE FACULTY OF IMAGINING AS ONE'S OWN THE SUFFERING AND JOY OF OTHERS.

ANDRE GIDE

FRENCH NOVELIST

JESUS THE ANARCHIST

ONE OF THE BEST-KEPT SECRETS OF THE WORLD HAS BEEN THE ACTIVISM—THE NONVIOLENT RESISTANCE—OF JESUS. A CLOSE READING OF THE GOSPEL REVEALS HIS CALLING TO ACCOUNT AN UNJUST, CORRUPT SYSTEM.

KINDNESS DOES NOT ADEQUATELY DESCRIBE HIS RELATIONSHIP TO THE POOR OR TO THOSE WHO SUFFER. COMPASSION IS BETTER. "MY HEART IS MOVED WITH COMPASSION FOR THE CROWD, BECAUSE THEY HAVE BEEN WITH ME NOW FOR THREE DAYS AND HAVE NOTHING TO EAT." (MARK 8:2) NOR DOES NONVIOLENT REVOLUTIONARY SUM HIM UP. ANARCHIST IS BETTER: ONE WHO LIVES SELF-GOVERNMENT, REPRE-SENTING THE POOR, RESISTING A CRIMINAL STATE, AND ATTENDING TO THE JUST WORKS OF GOD. "THEN REPAY TO CAESAR WHAT BELONGS TO CAESAR, AND TO GOD WHAT BELONGS TO GOD." (MATTHEW 22:21) SINCE ALL BELONGED TO GOD, HE GAVE NOTHING TO CAESAR.

MOST OF THE REFERENCES TO JESUS' KINDNESS AND ANTIVIOLENCE ARE SUPPRESSED TODAY, SIMPLY BECAUSE THE ESTABLISHED CHURCH HAS CHOSEN CHAPLAINCY TO THE IMPERIAL STATE. VIRTUALLY NO ONE

TEACHES CHRISTIANS THE NONVIOLENCE OF JESUS, NOR HIS CALLING TO COMMUNITY, NOR HIS VOLUNTARY POVERTY, NOR HIS CHOICE OF THE CROSS. ESPECIALLY HIS CHOICE OF THE CROSS, THAT LIVING SYMBOL OF RESISTANCE TO EVIL, INCLUDING SYSTEMIC EVIL—RESISTANCE TO IMPERIAL GOVERNMENTS, TO PREDATORY CORPORATIONS, TO NUCLEAR WEAPONS, TO WAR, TO THE DESPOLIATION OF THE ENVIRON-MENT, TO KILLING IN ANY FORM.

WHAT ARE THESE ORGANIZATIONS OF OPPRESSION THAT LIE TO US, ROB US, AND SOMETIMES KILL US? EMPIRES, NATION-STATES, GLOBALIZED CORPORATIONS, WORLD TRADE ORGANIZATIONS, TARIFF AND TRADE AGREEMENTS (NAFTA), WAR MINISTRIES (DEPARTMENT OF DEFENSE), BANKS, STOCK EXCHANGES. JESUS WOULD DENOUNCE AND RESIST THE SCURRYING, BLIND CREATURES THAT BUILD AND IDOLIZE THEM, WHILE LOVING THEM AND AGONIZING OVER THEIR CONVERSION.

PHILIP BERRIGAN

CATHOLIC ANTIWAR AND ANTINUCLEAR ACTIVIST

TRY THIS

BEGINNING TODAY, TREAT EVERYONE YOU MEET AS IF THEY WERE GOING TO BE DEAD BY MIDNIGHT. EXTEND TO THEM ALL THE CARE, KINDNESS, AND UNDERSTANDING YOU CAN MUSTER, AND DO IT WITH NO THOUGHT OF ANY REWARD. YOUR LIFE WILL NEVER BE THE SAME AGAIN.

OG MANDINO

U.S. AUTHOR, SELF-HELP GURU

WHAT WOULD THE WORLD BE LIKE IF WE WERE KINDER TO OUR CHILDREN?

TEACHING KINDNESS

LET'S HELP OUR CHILDREN DEVELOP THE HABIT OF FREEDOM, AND ENCOURAGE THEM TO CELEBRATE WHO AND WHAT THEY ARE.

LET'S STOP TEACHING CHILDREN TO FEAR CHANGE AND TO PROTECT THE STATUS QUO. LET'S TEACH THEM TO INQUIRE AND DEBATE, TO ASK QUESTIONS UNTIL THEY HEAR ANSWERS. THE WAY TO DO THAT IS TO CHANGE TRADITIONAL SCHOOLING.

OUR EDUCATIONAL SYSTEM DOES ITS BEST TO IGNORE AND SUPPRESS THE CREATIVE SPIRIT OF CHILDREN. IT TEACHES THEM TO LISTEN UNQUESTIONINGLY TO AUTHORITY. IT INSISTS THAT EDUCATION IS JUST STOCKPILING KNOWLEDGE, AND THAT THE PURPOSE OF EDUCA-TION IS TO GET A JOB. WHAT'S LEFT OUT IS SENSITIVITY TO OTHERS,

NONVIOLENT BEHAVIOR, RESPECT, INTUITION, IMAGINATION AND A SENSE OF AWE AND WONDERMENT.

IF WE DEVELOP A MORAL SENSITIVITY THAT CONSISTS OF CARE RATHER THAN COERCION MAYBE THE PRACTICES THAT HAVE LED TO ECONOMIES THAT USE MILLIONS OF CHILD LABORERS, ARMIES THAT TURN KIDS INTO KILLERS, AND A SOCIETY IN WHICH CHILD PROSTITUTION IS ONE OF THE FASTEST GROWING INDUSTRIES WILL END.

ANITA RODDICK, OBE

ACTIVIST AND FOUNDER, THE BODY SHOP

YOU NEVER FORGET PEOPLE WHO WERE KIND TO YOU WHEN YOU WERE YOUNG.

MARK BIRLEY   BRITISH RESTAURATEUR

blessing,

YOUTH

hopes

fun

IMAGINA

TRUTH

learning

dreaming

THE IDEAS THAT HAVE LIGHTED MY WAY HAVE BEEN KINDNESS, BEAUTY AND TRUTH.

ALBERT EINSTEIN

A NEW KIND OF KINDNESS

EVEN AT AGE 10, IT SEEMED SENTIMENTALLY MAWKISH TO ME WHEN, IN THE CRAZE FOR FILLING AUTOGRAPH BOOKS, MY FATHER MADE HIS CONTRIBUTION TO MINE: "LIFE IS MOSTLY FROTH AND BUBBLE/TWO THINGS STAND LIKE STONE/KINDNESS IN ANOTHER'S TROUBLE/COURAGE IN YOUR OWN."

WHEN COMPARING THE COLLECTION WITH FRIENDS, I QUICKLY SKIPPED OVER TO MORE HUMOROUS ENTRIES. POSTWAR, COASTAL, SUBURBAN AUSTRALIANS LIVED FOR THE BEACH, SUNSHINE, ACTIVITY, FRIENDSHIP, THE GOOD LIFE. HEDONISM RULED, IF CHECKED BY A GENERAL SENTI-MENT THAT THE UNDERDOG SHOULD TRIUMPH AND THE VAGUE PHILOSOPHY OF FAIR-DO'S FOR ALL.

THE MATURE CONSCIENCE OF THE POSTWAR GENERATION GLOBALLY DROPPED DO-GOODING IN FAVOR OF ANALYSIS AND INSIGHT INTO SOCIAL AND POLITICAL STRUCTURES THAT MAINTAIN INEQUALITY AND GENERATE INJUSTICE. KINDNESS DID NOT FIT INTO THE ANALYSIS. BEING

KIND WAS FOR ANIMALS, CHILDREN, THE ELDERLY, YOURSELF EVEN, AND MAYBE THE ENVIRONMENT. KINDNESS WAS TOO BANAL FOR THE BIG SOCIAL ISSUES. KINDNESS WAS FOR PRIVATE, PERSONAL ACTIONS. YET ONE OF THE MAJOR SOCIAL MOVEMENTS OF THE SECOND HALF OF THE 20TH CENTURY FOUGHT FIERCELY FOR RECOGNITION THAT THE PERSONAL IS POLITICAL. SO IS IT TIME FOR A NEW KIND OF KINDNESS?

WHAT MESSAGE WOULD I GIVE MY CHILDREN? TAKE OUT THE SENTI-MENTALITY, KEEP THE SENTIMENT. IN A WORLD OF PLENTY, THE KINDNESS TEST SHOULD STAND LIKE STONE.

BARBARA DINHAM

DIRECTOR, PESTICIDE ACTION NETWORK, UK

**NO ACT OF KINDNESS, NO MATTER HOW SMALL,
IS EVER WASTED.**

AESOP

HOSTILITY EVAPORATES

ALBERT SCHWEITZER SAID, "CONSTANT KINDNESS CAN ACCOMPLISH MUCH. AS THE SUN MAKES ICE MELT, KINDNESS CAUSES MISUNDER-STANDING, MISTRUST, AND HOSTILITY TO EVAPORATE."

KINDNESS SOFTENS THE ARMOR OF MAN. IT SOOTHES THE HEART AND CREATES A PLACE OF COMFORT AND SAFETY. ACTS OF KINDNESS CAN CHANGE OUR STATE OF MIND FROM FEAR-BASED ANGER AND AGGRES-SION TO A FEELING OF ACCEPTANCE, TRANQUILITY AND PEACE.

WE HUMANS HAVE THE CAPACITY TO CHANGE THE WORLD WITH ACTS OF LOVE AND KINDNESS. LET'S START BY TEACHING OUR CHILDREN THE IMPORTANCE OF COMPASSION. YOUTH ARE THE INHERITORS OF THIS PLANET AND ALL ITS POTENTIAL. THE ACT OF EXPOSING OUR LITTLE ONES TO HIGHER TEACHINGS OF LOVING KINDNESS WILL GIVE THEM THE CORRECT TOOLS TO CONSTRUCT A MORE TOLERANT AND PEACEFUL WORLD.

I HAVE WITNESSED THE SOFTENING OF THE HARDEST OF HEARTS BY A SIMPLE SMILE. HUMAN KINDNESS CAN TURN ARMAMENTS INTO ARMISTICE.

GOLDIE HAWN   **AMERICAN ACTRESS**

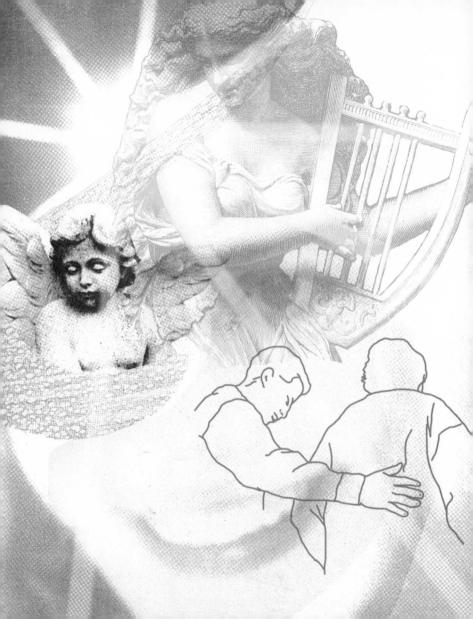

HIDDEN TREASURES

THE AMERICAN ANARCHIST EMMA GOLDMAN SAID, "NO ONE HAS YET FULLY REALIZED THE WEALTH OF SYMPATHY, KINDNESS AND GENEROSITY HIDDEN IN THE SOUL OF A CHILD. THE EFFORT OF EVERY TRUE EDUCATION SHOULD BE TO UNLOCK THAT TREASURE."

I THINK WE TEND TO UNDERESTIMATE THE INTELLIGENCE AND DEPTH OF OUR CHILDREN. OUR WAY OF SCHOOLING IS ARCHAIC. AS WE EVOLVE AS PEOPLE, WE MUST ALSO ENHANCE THE WAY WE EDUCATE OUR LITTLE ONES. I KNOW THAT MINE ARE MUCH SMARTER THAN ME. I WANT TO UNLOCK THEIR BEAUTIFUL BRAINS AND EXPOSE THOSE TREASURES.

MELANIE GRIFFITH

AMERICAN ACTRESS

MY RELIGION IS VERY SIMPLE. MY RELIGION IS KINDNESS.

THE DALAI LAMA

CONTRIBUTORS

ADRIANA DE GASPAR DE ALBA is the former head franchisee for The Body Shop Mexico, and the mother of three.

PETER BASHFORD is the chairman and founder of Maiti Children's Trust, a U.K.-based charity that combats the trafficking of Nepali women and children into sexual slavery in India and the Gulf states. Peter is a researcher on HIV and AIDS in these communities. The Trust has set up a number of projects including a hospice for AIDS victims in India and Nepal. **maiti.info@btinternet.com** or **www.maitinepal.com**

PHILIP BERRIGAN was the first priest in the world to be arrested for political dissent. With his brother Daniel, he spent most of his 79 years opposing war and nuclear weapons with the ecumenical pacifist group Plowshares. In 1968, the Berrigan brothers were arrested for setting American draft files on fire using homemade napalm in protest against the Vietnam war. Philip and Daniel were twice nominated for the Nobel Peace Prize. By the time of his death in December 2002, Philip had spent a total of more than 11 years in federal prison for nonviolent civil disobedience.

JOHN BIRD is the co-founder of *The Big Issue*, a news and current-affairs magazine written by professional journalists and sold on the streets by homeless vendors. Bird is also president of The Big Issue Foundation Board of Trustees. **www.bigissue.co.uk.**

ROBERT CAPRINI-WOOD is a job-skills trainer focusing on enhancing the employability of refugees. He is a member of the Chartered Institute of Personnel and Development. **www.cipd.org.uk**

BARBARA DINHAM is the director of Pesticide Action Network U.K., which works to reduce the health and environmental hazards of pesticides and to promote sustainable alternatives in the United Kingdom, Europe and developing countries, particularly Africa. **www.pan-uk.org**

SCILLA ELWORTHY is the director of the Oxford Research Group, which she founded in 1982 to investigate the policies of the five major nuclear nations. The Oxford Group brings together defense officials from these nations and their critics to discuss disarmament. Elworthy has twice been nominated for the Nobel Peace Prize, and recently won the Niwano Peace Prize. **www.oxfordresearchgroup.org.uk**

SCOTT FLEMING is a criminal-defense and human-rights attorney based in

Oakland, California. He is a native of Florida and a 1999 law graduate of the University of California at Berkeley. He has worked on behalf of prisoners, including Albert Woodfox and Herman Wallace of the Angola 3, throughout his career. www.angola3.org.

MATTHEW FOX is a spiritual theologian and author of 25 books including *The Reinvention of Work, Original Blessing, Sins of the Spirit, Blessings of the Flesh, A Spirituality Named Compassion* and *Creativity: Where the Divine and the Human Meet*. He is the founder and president of the University of Creation Spirituality in Oakland, California, and co-director of the Naropa University master's degree program in creation spirituality. He sponsors monthly "Techno Cosmic Masses" to revitalize worship through dance and multimedia. www.creationspirituality.org and www.matthewfoxfcs.org

JUSTIN FRANCIS is the co-founder of Responsibletravel.com and its sister publication *The Responsible Traveller*, which offer the world's largest selection of "holidays that give the world a break." Holidays range from walking holidays in France, to stays on organic farms in the U.K., luxury hotels on the Indian Ocean, swimming with humpback whales in Fiji, and volunteering to help street children in Ecuador. All the holidays have been screened to ensure that they benefit local communities and to minimize negative social and environmental impacts. www.responsibletravel.com

JOHN FREDERICK is the editor of *Fallen Angels: The Sex Workers of South Asia*. He has lived and worked in South Asia for the last 15 years and is the director of Ray of Hope, an organization allied against sex trafficking, child prostitution, forced prostitution, gender aggression, domestic violence and sexual abuse. Ray of Hope provides consultancy in research, intervention design and planning, and human resources development for local, national and international organizations. www.rayhope.org.

JEFF GATES is the founder of the Shared Capitalism Institute, an organization dedicated to making free enterprise more equitable and sustainable. He is the author of *The Ownership Solution: Toward a Shared Capitalism for the Twenty-First Century* and *Democracy at Risk: Rescuing Main Street from Wall Street*. Gates was formerly a counsel to the U.S. Senate Committee on Finance. www.sharedcapitalism.org

LESLIE GEORGE is a journalist based in New York. She has written for several national magazines and formerly worked as a producer at Pacifica radio, including several years with WBAI in

CONTRIBUTORS

New York. In 1996, she won the Silver Reel from the National Federation of Community Broadcasters for her documentary "Drug Mules." She currently produces and reports for Free Speech Radio News. **www.fsrn.org**

SHAKS GHOSH is the chief executive of Crisis, a homeless services organization in the United Kingdom. She earned an MSc in Urban Studies, Ghosh has held a number of jobs in local government and the voluntary housing movement. Crisis develops innovative services which enable their homeless clients to overcome addictions and mental health issues, learn social and practical skills, join the world of work and reintegrate into society. **www.crisis.org.uk**

MELANIE GRIFFITH is a well-known Hollywood actress and mother of three. She is the honorary co-president of the SABERA Foundation based in Calcutta, India, and co-founder of the Internet company OneWorldLive. With husband Antonio Banderas, she founded Green Moon, an entertainment production company. **www.melaniegriffith.com** and **www.oneworldlive.com**

JAY HARRIS is the publisher of *Mother Jones* magazine, a progressive, independent magazine of public interest investigative reporting. Since its founding in 1976, *Mother Jones* has won virtually

every award available to magazines, while consistently irritating the powers that be in business and government. **www.motherjones.com.**

GOLDIE HAWN is a well-known, well-loved, Academy Award-winning actress. In addition to her prolific career in entertainment, Goldie is devoted to her family and to countless humanitarian endeavors, both public and private.

WAYNE HEMINGWAY is the co-founder of the highly successful fashion design studio Red or Dead, which won the British Fashion Council's Street Style Designer of the Year award three times in a row in the 1990s. **www.redordead.com**

DAVID HIGGS is the founder of The Environmental Press Agency. A photographer, writer and outdoorsman, Higgs was born and raised in Australia but now lives in Britain. An experienced mountaineer, diver and all-round adventurer, he has made notable climbs in the Himalayas, and made the first-ever descent of the Zambezi River from Victoria Falls to Lake Kariba by inflatable raft. As a photographer, he has worked for *Life* magazine, *Sports Illustrated* and *National Geographic*. He has also written extensively on a wide variety of issues ranging from human rights to conservation, wilderness and the environment. His exposé on child slave labor in Indonesia won the top prize in the 2000 Human Rights Press Awards sponsored by Amnesty International. In 2001, he was awarded an MBE for services to the environment and photo-journalism.

REBECCA ALBAN HOFFBERGER is the founder and director of the American Visionary Art Museum in Baltimore. **www.avam.org**

JACOB HOLDT is a Danish vagabond and documentary photographer who has spent the last three decades hitch-hiking throughout the United States. He arrived with less than $40 and sold his blood twice a week to buy film. He has lived with hundreds of families, from the poorest migrant workers to America's wealthiest families such as the Rockefellers. Along the way, he joined the Native American rebellion in Wounded Knee, infiltrated secret Ku Klux Klan meetings and the Republican presidential campaign headquarters. The photos from his adventures are now part of a multimedia show called American Pictures, which has been shown in 14 countries. **www.american-pictures.com**

CARL JENSEN is the founder of Project Censored and a former professor of communications at Sonoma State University in California. He is the author of *Stories That Changed America*, and numerous books on censorship. Each year, Project Censored honors the 10 most important public-interest news stories that were ignored by the mainstream media. **www.projectcensored.org**

ANGELINA JOLIE won the Academy Award for Best Actress in a Supporting Role for the movie *Girl, Interrupted*. She is currently serving as a Goodwill Ambassador for the United Nations High Commissioner for Refugees high-lighting the human cost of the conflict around the world. **www.unhcr.ch**

MARIA JOSE LUBERTINO is an Argentine women's human-rights defender, lawyer, politician and journal-ist. She is a professor of Human Rights at Buenos Aires University Law School, and president of the Social and Political Women's Institute in Argentina.

CHARLES KERNAGHAN is the executive director of the National Labor Committee in Support of Human and Worker Rights. He and the NLC are perhaps best known for exposing the use of child labor in the production of Wal-Mart's "Kathie Lee" clothing line. Through public education and action campaigns focused on U.S. multination-als including Wal-Mart, Disney, GAP, Liz

CONTRIBUTORS

Claiborne and others, Kernaghan and the NLC have succeeded in raising public awareness of the sweatshop issue and engaging the U.S. people in a growing campaign to protect the fundamental human rights of workers who make the products we buy. **www.nlcnet.org**

DAVID KORTEN is board chair of the Positive Futures Network, which publishes *YES! Magazine*, president of the People-Centered Development Forum, and author of *When Corporations Rule the World* and *The Post-Corporate World: Life After Capitalism*. **www.davidkorten.org, www.futurenet.org**, and **www.developmentforum.net**

ANNIE LENNOX is a working mother and a Grammy Award–winning, internationally acclaimed musician, singer and songwriter. In December 2002 she was presented with The Century Award, *Billboard's* highest honor for distinguished creative achievement. **www.annie-lennox.com**

PETER LUCE is a hospital medical director. He recommends two U.K.-based organizations for cancer information and local referrals: the Cancer BACUP national information service at **www.cancerbacup.org.uk**; and Macmillan Cancer Relief at **www.macmillan.org.uk**.

KATE MAHER-PURCELL was pregnant with her second daughter when her husband Greg was diagnosed with pancreatic cancer on her 28th birthday, in February 2001. From that moment, their journey consisted of hospitals and surgeries, ultimately returning home to spend the last year of their lives together. Greg died on March 5, 2002, at home next to his daughters, surrounded by friends and family.

MARILYN MATHEW is a Jungian analyst working with adults in private practice in Dulwich, south London where she lives with her family. She is a full member of the British Association of Psychotherapists for which conducts professional training programs. She also teaches at Birkback University. **www.bap-psychotherapy.org**

RALPH NADER is a consumer advocate, lawyer and author. He has founded numerous public-interest organizations, including the Center for Study of Responsive Law, the Public Interest Research Group, the Clean Water Action Project, the Disability Rights Center, Public Citizen, and the magazine *Multinational Monitor*. In 1996 and 2000, he ran for President of the United States on the Green Party ticket. **www.nader.org** and **www.essential.org**

MISTY OLDLAND is a singer, songwriter and owner of MisticDiscs, an independent label in the United Kingdom. She will be releasing her third album "Forest Soul" in 2003. **www.mistyoldland.com** and **www.misticdiscs.com**

DAVID ORR is the author of *The Nature of Design* and *Earth in Mind*, and professor of environmental studies at Oberlin College in Ohio.

VICTOR PACE is a native of Malta who has lived in Britain since 1989. He trained in palliative care at St. Christopher's Hospice in London and worked in a number of hospices in southern England, coming back to St Christopher's as a consultant in 1999. He divides his time between work in the hospice inpatient unit and in community care facilities. He specializes in the care of patients with cancer of the head and neck, which often affects patients' appearance and social relationships.

ALWYN PEREIRA is the chief executive of Youth Entertainment Studios U.K. and a social entrepreneur, developing new forms of educational systems to empower young people. **www.yestudios.com**

PETER PHILLIPS is the director of Project Censored, and an associate professor and department chair of sociology at Sonoma State University in California. Each year, Project Censored honors the 10 most important public-interest news stories that were ignored by the mainstream media. **www.projectcensored.org**

WARREN PUCKETT is a two-time Distinguished Honor Graduate of the Defense Language Institute for study in German and Spanish. In his 15-year career in the U.S. Army, and was a decorated officer, combat veteran and member of the Special Forces Command. He left the Army in 1994 when it became clear that the government he served did not share his sense of honorable humanity. Today, he is the associate director of the Fifty Crows Foundation, a non-profit organization dedicated to using documentary photography to bring attention to injustices around the world. **www.fiftycrows.org**

AMY RAY and EMILY SALIERS are the Indigo Girls, a Grammy Award-winning folk duo. With Winona LaDuke, they founded Honor the Earth, a native environmental rights organization. They describe themselves as activists first and musicians second. Ray is also the founder of Daemon Records, an independent label based in Atlanta, Georgia. **www.indigogirls.com**, **www.honorearth.org**, and **www.daemonrecords.com**

CONTRIBUTORS

LINUS ROACHE is an actor whose films include *Priest*, *Wings of the Dove*, *Pandaemonium* and *Beyond Borders*. He has dedicated his life to a revolution in human consciousness, inspired by the vision and life of spiritual teacher and evolutionary philosopher Andrew Cohen. **www.andrewcohen.org**

VANDANA SHIVA is an activist, physicist, ecologist, and feminist. She founded the Research Foundation for Science, Technology & Ecology, an organization dedicated to defending resources and biodiversity in India and the Third World. She also started Navdanya, a grassroots movement for the conservation of biodiversity. She is a founding member of the International Forum on Globalization. She has written numerous books including *Water Wars*, *Stolen Harvest*, *Biopiracy*, and *Monoculture of the Mind*. In 1993, she won The Right Livelihood Award, often called the "alternative Nobel Prize." **www.vshiva.net**

TINA SCHLIESKE is a singer, songwriter, and recording artist based in Minneapolis and California. Her band, Tina and the B-Sides, has released six albums, including "It's All Just the Same" on the Sire Records label. **www.tinabsides.com**

WILLIAM STUEBNER is a former U.S. Army major and the executive director of the Institute for International Criminal Investigations. As an international observer for peacekeeping, he has worked in El Salvador, the Balkans and Chechnya. **www.iici.info**

JOS STRENGHOLT is the general manager of Mediahouse Egypt, which specializes in Arabic-language video production for organizations doing business in Egypt and Sudan. A native of The Netherlands, he studied the history of the Middle East at university in Utrecht. He lives in Egypt with his wife and three daughters. **www.mediahouse.org**

LAZARUS TAMANA is the president of the Movement for the Survival of the Ogoni People. MOSOP was formed in 1990 in response to decades of environmental devastation and human-rights violations perpetrated against the Ogoni people of the Niger delta by major transnational oil companies, particularly Royal Dutch Shell, with the help of the corrupt military regime in Nigeria. Lazarus is also on the board of trustees of the Ogoni Foundation, a U.K.-registered charity founded in 1995. **mosop@gn.apc.org** and **laz@ogonifoundation.org**

DAVID TOVEY is a general practitioner from South London. He works in a large group practice within the National Health Service. He is also tutors other physicians in their post-graduate studies.

WILL TRAVERS is CEO of The Born Free Foundation, an international wildlife charity. Travers' father Bill and Virginia McKenna established the foundation after starring in the classic film *Born Free*. Today, Born Free works worldwide to prevent the abuse and exploitation of wild animals, and to conserve threat-ened species. Will is particularly devoted to the plight of captive animals and the protection of elephants. He is also resident of the Species Survival Network, and a fellow of the Royal Geographic Society. **www.bornfree.org.uk**

HERMAN WALLACE and ALBERT WOODFOX are political prisoners at the Louisiana State Penitentiary at Angola. With Robert King Wilkerson, who was freed in 2000, they are known as the Angola Three. In the early 1970s, Angola prison—a former slave planta-tion—was known as the "most brutal prison in America." The administration was corrupt and racist; and murder, rape, and sexual slavery were a part of everyday life inside. Wallace and Woodfox, members of the Black Panther Party, attempted to organize their fellow prisoners against the corruption and racism of the prison administration and in defense of weaker prisoners who were often exploited or killed. Threatened by their activism, the prison administration and the state framed the men for the 1972 murder of a white prison guard. The men have been held in solitary confinement for more than 30 years. **www.angola3.org** and **www.anitaroddick.com/angola**

THE BIG ISSUE VENDORS (JOHN SHEEHY, PAMELA, SAM, AND JOHN C.) *The Big Issue* is a news and current affairs magazine written by professional journalists and sold on the streets by homeless vendors. **www.bigissue.co.uk**

get **informed,**
get **outraged,**
get **inspired,**
get **active!**

WWW

AnitaRoddick.com

AnitaRoddick.com is eclectic, full of personal essays, quirky links, breaking news, and activist information. Updated regularly, Anita's site is vital and well-regarded within the weblogging community.

Whether she is filing dispatches from the Amazon rainforest, or soliciting tongue-in-cheek spoofs of corporate logos, or pillorying world leaders for their war-like ways, Anita's website is a peek into the mind of a woman, an entrepreneur, an activist, a grandmother, a curious and concerned global citizen. It is full of joy and passion, outrage and information.

More than just an autobiography or a book about business, Roddick also addresses personal issues such as self-esteem, and wider political issues such as the human-rights abuses associated with economic globalization. The Body Shop is one of the business success stories of the century. This book tells you how and why.

THE STORY OF A MAVERICK WHO CHANGED THE FACE OF BUSINESS.

BUSINESS AS UNUSUAL

Anita Roddick is one of the world's most outspoken, controversial, and successful businesswomen. *Business as Unusual* charts the story of Roddick and her company, The Body Shop, through the lows and highs of the last decade. Along the way, she turns the tables on the way society looks at business and shows how it is possible for an international company to act ethically, responsibly, and accountably, without sacrificing good business sense or profit margin.

ISBN: 0-7225-3987-8
Retail Price: U.K. £7.99, U.S. $24.95